D1871556

ENGLISH DICTIONARY SENTENCES GRAMMAR AND PRONUNCIATION

English Dictionary Sentences Grammar and Pronunciation

P. V. GOPALAKRISHNAN

KALPAZ PUBLICATIONS
Delhi-110052

English Dictionary Sentences Grammar and Pronunciation

ISBN: 81-7835-310-5

© P. V. Gopalakrishnan

All rights reserved. No part of this book may be reproduced in any manner without written permission.

Published in 2015 in India by
Kalpaz Publications,
C-30, Satyawati Nagar, Delhi-110052
E-mail : Kalpaz@hotmail.com

Laser Typesetting at : Shiva Infosystem, Delhi
Printed at : Mehra Offset Press, Delhi

Contents

HOME STUDY SERIES - 1

SPELLING AND VOCABULARY

P. V. GOPALAKRISHNAN

SPELLING

HOME STUDY SERIES - 0

USING THE DICTIONARY

P. V. GOPALAKRISHNAN

CONTENTS

Sl. No.	Chapters	Exercise written date	Re-written date	Marks	Remarks
1.	Chapter - 1				
2.	Chapter - 2				
3.	Chapter - 3				
4.	Chapter - 4				
5.	Chapter - 5				
6.	Chapter - 6				
7.	Chapter - 7				
8.	Chapter - 8				
9.	Chapter - 9				
10.	Chapter - 10				
11.	Chapter - 11				
12.	Chapter - 12				
13.	Chapter - 13				
14.	Chapter - 14				
15.	Chapter - 15				
16.	Chapter - 16				

CONTENTS

Sl. No.	Chapters	Exercise written date	Re-written date	Marks	Remarks
17.	Chapter - 17				
18.	Chapter - 18				
19.	Chapter - 19				
20.	Chapter - 20				
21.	Chapter - 21				
22.	Chapter - 22				

1

Featuers of a Good Dictionary

A dictionary is a book, which gives word meanings of a language. The words in it are arranged in alphabetical order. Dictionary is an important tool in the study of a language.

There are many types of dictionaries available in the book market.

How can we select a good one from them? A good dictionary is not the one, which is attractive in sight or large in number of pages. Students are advised not to be deceived by the advertisements of booksellers and publishers.

Check if the following qualities can be seen in the dictionary, which you propose to buy.

(a) At least one lakhs of entries — A dictionary having at least one lakhs of entries is considered useful for a student. Concise dictionaries do not give neither detailed meanings nor contain rarely used words.

(b) Different meanings of a word — A word may have many meanings. Only a good dictionary gives all the meaning. A concise or a bad dictionary gives only the main meaning, and ignores the other meanings.

(c) Encyclopaedic references— A good dictionary gives a brief explanation of important places, persons, things and ideas.

(d) Illustrations— Some foreign things, animals or plants cannot be understood however it is explained in words. If the picture of the same is given, it can be digested very easily. Good dictionaries possess illustrations.

(e) All the other forms of a word— In addition to the meaning a good dictionary gives all the other forms of the word such as adjective, adverb, noun and verb. This would be a great help as students often face difficulty to find adjectival form, adverbal form, noun form or verbal form of a particular word.

(f) Phrases and idioms— Phrases and idioms differ a great deal in meaning compared to the lexical meaning of the words in it. Hence meanings of phrases and idioms should be given separately. A good dictionary does it.

(g) Pronunciation— English pronunciation is a difficult thing for Indian students. It is because many phonemes in English are alien to Indian language. A good dictionary gives in brackets the pronunciation of each entry.

(h) Stress— English stresses are situational. Stress positions may change in inflected and affixed forms of a word. This will not make a difficult matter to a user of a good dictionary.

(i) Abbreviated forms— In English some abbreviations such as NATO, AIDS etc. are familiar. A good dictionary explains what these things are.

(j) Foreign words and phrases— Foreign words such as 'Alma mater', 'Agenda', 'Tour de force' are a part of the English vocabulary. A good dictionary gives the meanings of them also.

(k) Word origin— Though this is unnecessary for a beginner, a little knowledge of how a word originated will do good. Some good dictionaries would tell this also.

(l) Bi-linguality in nature— For a beginner bi-lingual dictionaries are better. It explains the meaning both in English and in vernacular language. However it is advised to understand English words in English meaning.

(m) Good binding— A good dictionary possesses a neat and hard binding. Otherwise the pages would get untied in a few weeks' use. In addition to the above mentioned qualities of a good dictionary, there are two more points to be remembered when you deal with dictionaries.

Always keep a pocket or concise dictionary along with the dictionary that has the above-mentioned qualities. If you use the big dictionary every now and then, the big one would get damaged. In order to avoid it you are advised to consult the big one only when you fail to locate a word in the concise one.

There are a few American dictionaries in the book market. They are quite different from that of the British ones. As we are following British spellings and meanings, it will be better to ignore the American ones and think of British dictionaries.

Dictionaries normally do not give antonyms of words. For getting antonyms and synonyms of words consult a Thesaurus.

EXERCISES

Q: Write down the qualities of your dictionary.

Ans:

Chapter- 2

We have already discussed that the words in a dictionary are arranged in the alphabetical order. A beginner should get a little knowledge on where should look for a particular word. This knowledge can be acquired through practice.

Let us see how the letters in each of the following groups are rearranged in the alphabetical order.

(a) w, b, c, a
(b) p, m, v, d
(c) r, k, s, f

Look at the first group of the letters. The letter 'a' comes first in the alphabetical order compared to the other letters. Then comes 'b'. Next 'c' and 'w' at the last. So, that group may be re-arranged like a, b, c, w.

In the second group of letters 'd' comes first compared to the other three. Next comes 'm', 'p', and 'v' are behind 'm' respectively. Hence this group may be re-arranged as d, m, p, v.

The last group, as seen above, may be re-arranged as: f, k, r, s.

EXERCISES

Q. Re-arrange the following groups of letters in the alphabetical order.

(a) p, t, u, f
(b) s, g, v, w
(c) m, o, k, t
(d) x, d, l, q
(e) c, a, r, o
(f) h, b, n, f
(g) i, n, t, g
(h) j, h, d, n
(i) o, v, d, f
(j) r, m, b, a

Ans:

(a)	(b)	(c)
(d)	(e)	(f)
(g)	(h)	(i)
(j)		

Chapter-3

Words are also re-arranged in the same manner as we seen earlier. For example look at the following group of words

cat, bad, man.

At first consider the first letters of each word. They are 'c', 'b', and 'm'.

In this group 'b' comes first in the alphabetical order. It is followed by 'c' and 'm' respectively. Hence the group of words may re-arranged as: bad, cat, man.

Here are some other groups. Look at them,

(a) wood, work, what, water.

(b) hit, hat, hot, hut

(c) did, dead, deep, door.

The first letter of the words given in the first group is same. Then how can we rearrange them? There is nothing to worry. If the first letter is same, consider the second letter also. If the second letters are also same, consider third letter and so on. In the first group 'w' is the first letter of the all words. So we should consider the second letters. They are 'o', 'o', 'h' and 'a'. As 'a' comes first in the alphabetical order the word 'water' should come first in this group. Then comes 'what' as the second letter 'h' comes next in the alphabetical order. The second letters of 'wood' and 'work' are same. So we should consider the third letter of these two words. They are 'o' and 'r'. As 'o' comes first and 'r' comes last in the alphabetical order the word 'wood' comes third in the group and 'work' comes fourth.

In this way the above groups of words may be rearranged as:

(a) water, what, wood, work.

(b) hat, hit, hot, hut.

(c) dead, deep, did, door.

EXERCISE

1. Rearrange the words in each of the following groups in alphabetical order.

(a) can, could, take, beat

(b) boat, but, boot, bucket

(c) a, the, she, it, of

(d) what, which, where, when

(e) fool, food, foot, fuse

(f) neck, shoes, fail, neon

(g) handle, candle, bundle, mantle (h) chair, chance, chicken, chandran

(i) mouse, mat, meet, mock (j) Jill, Jack, Johny, Jose

(k) call, kill, hand, about (l) zero, seat, chain, X'mas

(m) bachelor, backward, baboon, ball

(n) deal, dead, danger, death.

Ans:

(a) (b)

(c) (d)

(e) (f)

(g) (h)

(i) (j)

(k) (l)

(m) (n)

2. Rearrange the words given in the following passage in alphabetical order.

We find many immoral people in our society. The youth of India must revolt against them. The by-gone generation has fought against all of them. We should lead noble ways of living to make this life useful to ourself and to the society. Actually this is cultural revolution.

Ans:

Chapter-4

In the endeavour of locating a word with the help of a dictionary, one should be tactful. If you know the first one or two letters of a word but do not know the word fully, you can find it with the help of a dictionary. It is only minor one among the many fold uses of a good dictionary. Here gives a few examples of the same. Go through them for learning that art.

Frame words using letters given in the first and second columns.

Q.

A	b	
	c	
	d	
	e	
	f	

Ans

A	b	About
	c	Acid
	d	Adjust
	e	Aerial
	f	Afraid

Frame words using letters given in the first, second and third columns.

Q.

D	i	c	
		e	
	u	s	
		u	
	r	p	
		a	

Ans.

D	i	c	Dictionary
		e	Diet
	u	s	Duel
		u	Dupe
	r	p	Drum
		a	Dragon

EXERCISE

Q. Frame meaningful words using letters given in the following columns.

(a) **Ans.**

S	p	
	o	
	i	
	t	
	a	
	w	
	n	
	u	

(b) **Ans.**

P	o	p	
		a	
	r	i	
		t	
	a	r	
		l	
	i	g	
		n	

Chapter-5

Here under gives some examples for filling up of the missed letters. You may find the missed letters with the help of a dictionary. Some examples are given for your ready reference.

Q. Supply with the missed letters

(a) w_rk
(b) ha_d
(c) b_nk
(d) than_
(e) th_n
(f) di_
(g) l_arn
(h) stud_
(i) scho_l
(j) _ou
(k) te_cher
(l) bo_k
(m) pe_

Ans: (a) work
(b) hand
(c) bank
(d) thank
(e) then
(f) did
(g) learn
(h) study
(i) school
(j) you
(k) teacher
(l) book
(m) pen

EXERCISE

Q. Supply with the missed letters.

(a) w—o
(b) th—t
(c) h_
(d) m_
(e) n_t
(f) go_d
(g) I__
(h) al_
(i) s_
(j) b_
(k) d_ _p
(l) h_r_
(m) m_ _
(o) p_op_ _
(p) m_
(q) c_l_

Ans:

(a)
(b)
(c)
(j)
(k)
(l)

(d)
(e)
(f)
(g)
(h)
(i)

(m)
(n)
(o)
(p)
(q)

Chapter-6

The following is another type of exercise. One word having one or more missed letters is given in the column A. Its meaning will be given in the column B. Find the word with the help of a dictionary.

A	B
Fe_ _ y	boat
Cu_t_m	habit
c_o_d	mass
j_urn_y	periodical
h_st_	hurry
a_ig_t	get down
k_ _	relative
gr_ _nd	earth's surface
f_ _th	belief
q_ _te	leave
s_n_ _	because

Ans:

ferry
custom
crowd
journal
haste
alight
ground
faith
quite
since
terror
kin

EXERCISE

Q. Write down the words given in the column A of the following supplying suitable letters. Meanings of the words are given in the column B.

A	B
pr_du__	yield
tr_ _l	examination
sin_ _re	genuine
pr_vi_ _onal	temporary
gu_t_r	a musical instrument
f_ _st	banquet
c_ _ple	two
b_ _n	something helpful
l_vy	impose tax
h_t	very small house

Ans:

A	B

Chapter-7

This section deals with rearrangement of letters to get meaningful words. Practicing this type of exercises would make you familiar with the spellings.

Q. Re-arrange the following letters to get meaningful words.

(1) IDNAI	(7) ENO
(2) ANC	(8) HTEY
(3) TTILEL	(9) ASW
(4) KAEM	(10) OG
(5) NADH	(11) TOU
(6) ROKW	(12) KATE

Ans:

(1) INDIA	(7) ONE
(2) CAN	(8) THEY
(3) LITTLE	(9) WAS
(4) MAKE	(10) GO
(5) HAND	(11) OUT
(6) WORK	(12) TAKE

EXERCISE

Q. Re-arrange the following letters to get meaningful words.

(1) RHEET	(8) OSN
(2) INDM	(9) CHSCOOL
(3) ENP	(10) REANL
(4) ROGUND	(11) OOKB
(5) RTEE	(12) YAW
(6) IVERR	(13) USB
(7) OONM	(14) OARD

Ans:

(1)	(8)
(2)	(9)
(3)	(10)
(4)	(11)
(5)	(12)
(6)	(13)
(7)	(14)

Chapter-8

In English one or two letters should be dropped, added or altered when suffixing. Look at the following examples. A good dictionary gives what changes should brought to the word for making its suffixed forms.

stop + ed → stopped
win + ing → winning
confer + ed → conferred
baby + plural 's' → babies
separate + ing → separating
apply + ed → applied
endure + able → endurable
cut + ing → cutting
pharmacy + ist → pharmacist
handle + ing → handling
endure + able → endurable
ferry + ed → ferried
file + ing → filing
immune + ity → immunity
race + ing → racing

EXERCISES

Q. Combine the followings. After combining the words together and check a dictionary to ensure that the spellings are correct.

(a) take + ing
(b) put + ing
(c) speak + able
(d) take + able
(e) remit + ed
(f) work + ed
(g) mango + plural 's'
(h) lady + plural 's'
(i) drive + er

Ans:

(a)
(b)
(c)
(d)
(e)
(f)
(g)
(h)
(i)

Chapter-9

The principal use of a dictionary is to know the meaning of words. A good dictionary gives situational meanings of words. When you look at a particular entry you have to go through all the meanings given against that word. The following examples show how situational the meanings of a word are.

Book	—	written, typed or printed pages bound together. Reserve ticket, seat or room
Do	—	Work at, effect, finish, provide, solve.
Free	—	Without cost, not restricted, loose, unoccupied.
Head	—	Chief, upper part of the body in which brain is kept.
Lead	—	Guide, persuade
Pass	—	Exceed, go by, transfer.
Save	—	Rescue, preserve for further.
Serve	—	Provide, work for another
Solve	—	Find answer, work out
Value	—	Utility, worth
X	—	Christian, cross.

EXERCISES

1. Write down all the meanings of the following words.
   (a) work
   (b) principal
   (c) chief
   (d) trial
   (e) handle

Ans:

(a)
(b)
(c)
(d)
(e)

2. Choose the correct definition from column B for the words given in column A.

A	B
Current	lowermost part
Visit	sudden flow
Triumph	call on
Fetch	call on
Bottom	great success
Grief	water or air in flow
Diphthong	bring using force

Ans :

A	B

Chapter-10

English pronunciations are hard to digest for Indian students. In order to make the pronunciation easy and correct, good dictionaries give pronunciation of each word in bracket against each entry. Students are advised to refer English pronouncing Dictionary for correct pronunciation. However a good dictionary can help you a great deal in this respect. Whenever you refer a dictionary for other purposes, it is better to look at the pronunciation also and try to pronounce it. This practice will be highly beneficial to you.

In dictionaries some symbols are used to make the pronunciation simple. Some of them are given below. As symbols vary from dictionary to dictionary only the famous ones are given below. Go through the introduction of the dictionary, which is in your possession. It would tell you whatever symbols are used in it and how they are used to make the pronunciation easier.

The symbols '—' given at the top of letter(s) is to show that it is a long sound.

E.g. N ā tion

T ea̅ ch

The symbol '◡' is used to indicate short sound.

E.g. Reŭqest, bŏŏk

The symbol '⌒' is used at the top of two letters to indicate that they have mixed sound.

E.g. c͡l ass

p͡l ant

The symbol '·' is used at the top of a letter to show that letter is silent.

E.g. ṗ sychology

ca ṙ pet

ma ṙ ket

endors ė

The symbol '·' is used at the bottom of a letter to show that the pronunciation of that letter is deviated a little from the familiar one.

Eg. carboḷic

almost
Sakthi

EXERCISE

1. Write down the pronunciations of the following words in your vernacular language.

(a) lord	(b) nation	(c) friend
(d) foreign	(e) sight	(f) laugh
(g) plantation	(h) bourgeois	(i) wool
(j) lieutenant	(k) sewing	(l) goal
(m) perplex	(n) satire	(o) rough
(p) comb	(q) care	(r) psychiatrist

Ans:

(a)	(b)	(c)
(d)	(e)	(f)
(g)	(h)	(i)
(j)	(k)	(l)
(m)	(n)	(o)
(p)	(q)	(r)

2. Find words in your dictionary having different spellings for 'f' and 'sh' sounds.

E.g. f → laugh, knife
sh → nation, fashion.

Ans:

3. Pick out a few words having the letter(s) 'r', 'o' or 'ph' and write their pronunciation in your mother tongue.

Ans:

Chapter-11

Apart from finding meanings and spellings of words dictionaries are used to find noun forms also. Take your dictionary and look at the word 'cancel'. At the end of its meaning the word 'cancellation' can also be seen with a 'n' before or after it. The 'n' is the short form of noun.

Compare the following examples with your dictionary and find how noun forms of a word can be found out from the dictionary.

succeed	—	success
brave	—	bravery
prepare	—	preparation
concentrate	—	concentration
commune	—	communism
national	—	nationality
incorporate	—	incorporation
neutral	—	neutrality
prefer	—	preferment
refuse	—	refusal
repay	—	repayment
transfuse	—	transfusion

EXERCISE

Q. Write noun forms of the followings:-

(a) read	(b) obey	(c) rectify	(d) social
(e) adult	(f) pharmacy	(g) fly	(h) bring
(i) revolve	(j) propagate	(k) oblige	(l) magnify
(m) lament	(n) intent	(o) incline	(p) graduate
(q) fail	(r) edit	(s) direct	(t) locate
(u) critical	(v) confer	(w) complicate	(x) advance
(y) accept	(z) abduct.		

Ans:

(a)	(b)	(c)	(d)
(e)	(f)	(g)	(h)
(i)	(j)	(k)	(l)
(m)	(n)	(o)	(p)
(q)	(r)	(s)	(t)
(u)	(v)	(w)	(x)
(y)	(z)		

Chapter-12

Like noun forms, verbal forms of words can also be found out using the dictionary. The symbol 'v' indicates verb. It is put before or after the verbal form. The dictionary also indicates that if the verb is transitive or intransitive, 'v.t' is used for showing transitive verb and 'v.i' is used for showing intransitive verb.

Given below are the few verbal forms. Compare it with your dictionary, and learn how to find verbal forms in your dictionary.

lamination — laminate
jogger — jog
fluoride — fluoridate
envious — envy
entrance — enter
doubtful — doubt
demonstration — demonstrate
conference — confer
compliance — comply
bomb — bombard

propagation — propagate
prediction — predict
severance — sever
sufferance — suffer
spectacle — spectate
severance — sever
red — redden
poster — post
population — populate
nipper — nip

A transitive verb is a verb which has a direct object. All the other verbs are in transitive. Normally dictionaries use the symbol 'v.t' for transitive verb and 'v.i' for intransitive verb. Some examples for transitive and intransitive verbs are given below. Compare these examples with your dictionary and learn how dictionaries give information about this.

mortify	—	transitive verb
offend	—	transitive verb
pertain	—	intransitive verb
chortle	—	intransitive verb
drive	—	transitive verb
ignore	—	transitive verb
laugh	—	intransitive verb
smile	—	intransitive verb
cower	—	intransitive verb
cluck	—	intransitive verb
waive	—	transitive verb

thrive — intransitive verb
mortify — transitive verb
launch — transitive verb
immerse — intransitive verb

We have already seen that words have noun and verbal forms. Meaning of a word differ greatly when used as a noun from that of the verbal usage. In some other cases there is no change in between verbal and noun forms. Examples for both are given below.

Some words which have same noun and verbal forms.

button	case
ferry	film
fortune	school

Examples for words, which possess a verbal meaning and a different meaning when, used as a noun.

face (n)	—	front part of head
,, (v)	—	turn
edge (n)	—	border
,, (v)	—	sharpen
cure (n)	—	heal
,, (v)	—	remedy

EXERCISES

1. Write at least ten verbs using your dictionary.

Ans: (a) (f)
(b) (g)
(c) (h)
(d) (i)
(e) (j)

2. Write verbal forms for the following words.

(a) isolation (e) personal
(b) equipment (f) commitment
(c) engagement (g) arrival
(d) criticism (h) reception

Ans: (a) (e)
(b) (f)
(c) (g)
(d) (h)

3. Write twelve words as examples for words having same noun and verbal forms.

Ans: (a) (g)
(b) (h)
(c) (i)
(d) (j)
(e) (k)
(f) (l)

4. Write twelve example for words having different meanings when used as noun and verb.

Ans: (a) (g)
(b) (h)
(c) (i)
(d) (j)
(e) (k)
(f) (l)

Chapter - 13

Adjective forms of words can also be seen in good dictionaries. The symbol used in dictionaries for adjectives is either 'a' or 'adj'. Look at the following words and try to locate them in your dictionary.

National
Provisional
Communal
Lexical
Red
Beautiful
Verbal

Another information that dictionaries give is the adverbial form, 'ad' or 'adv' is the symbol used in dictionaries for adverbial forms. Some examples are given below. Compare them with your dictionary.

Beautifull
Cordially
Legibly
Internationally
Utterly
Willingly

EXERCISES

1. Write ten adjectives.

Ans: (a) (b) (c) (d) (e) (f) (g) (h) (i) (j)

2. Write ten adverbs.

(a) (b) (c) (d) (e) (f) (g) (h) (i) (j)

3. Write adverbial and adjectival forms of the following words.

(a) nation (b) word

Ans: (a) (b)

Chapter-14

A phrase is a group of words, which gives a single meaning. Normally a phrase contains a main word and one or more minor words such as preposition, article etc. Pick out the main word and refer a dictionary. Then you can find the meaning of the same.

Look at the word 'call' in your dictionary. You may find phrases such as 'call on', 'call at', 'call up' etc.

Again, see the word 'get'. There you can see phrases such as get in, get out, get lost etc.

A few phrases are given below. The key word is underlined. Refer your dictionary to locate them.

In the middle of
Come by
Lost at
Water on
In between
Out of
Get in
Rule out
Make out
At home

EXERCISES

1. Find phrases from your dictionary having the following key words. Write their meanings also.

(a) go (b) get (c) come (d) look (e) went

Ans: (a)

(b)

(c)

(d)

(e)

2. Write meaning of the following phrases.

(a) turn over
(b) give in
(c) well off
(d) off and on
(e) in the long run
(f) in the soup
(g) bring home
(h) back out
(i) put up
(j) put out

Ans: (a)
(b)
(c)
(d)
(e)
(f)
(g)
(h)
(i)
(j)

Chapter-15

Almost all good dictionaries give a list of idioms in English at the end of it. Some dictionaries include it among the other entries. In such cases they can be found out by picking out the key words and locating them. Try to find out the meanings of the following idioms.

bad blood
hift of the gab
high spirits
mare's nest
give one's airs
pick up a row
burn the candle at both ends
black sheep
come to grief
bed of roses
smell a rat
die in harness
cook the accounts
dead letter
bed of thorns
have a finger in the pie

EXERCISE

1. Write down meanings of the following idioms.

(a) a dark horse (b) wild-goose chase
(c) set the Thames on fire (d) cold blood
(e) make a clean breast (f) high spirits
(g) keep pace with (h) sharp practice.

Ans: (a)
(b)
(c)
(d)
(e)
(f)
(g)
(h)

Chapter-16

There are a few words, which are prefixed in English. Important words among them will be given in the dictionary. Prefixes such as anti-, ante-, pre-, a-, for-, fore-, mother-, under-, over- etc. are used mainly. As they alter the meaning of the main word, a little knowledge of them would help you to find the meanings of the other words, which did not found way into the dictionary because of their unimportance. Try to find the following words in your dictionary.

pre-

- pre-degree
- pre-paid

fore-

- foresee
- forerunners

mother-

- motherland
- mother-tongue

over-

- overcome
- overhead

under-

- undertake
- underground

EXERCISE

Q. Write down as much as words that you can see in your dictionary having the following prefixes. Give their meanings also.

(a) hard (b) un (c) metal (d) cross (e) pseudo.

Ans:

(a)
(b)
(c)
(d)
(e)

Chapter-17

Like prefixes there are suffixes also like -ant, -er, -dom, -ist, -ice, -ian, -ism, -hood etc. They are used to make new words. Some examples are given below. Try to find them in your dictionary.

-ance
- hesitance
- inheritance

-room
- ballroom
- bedroom

-ous
- anxious
- superstitious

-ology
- zoology
- biology

-ify
- terrify
- purify

-handed
- left handed
- over handed

-ment
- judgment
- engagement

EXERCISE

Q. Write five examples for words having the following suffixes.

(a) –ly (b) –ance (c) –ension (d) –road (e) –tight (f) –dom

Ans: (a) (b)

(c) (d)

(e) (f)

Chapter-18

In English language there are a lot of pairs which have same pronunciation but different spellings. For your ready reference some examples are given in this section. Note the difference in meaning and spellings.

(1) cast – throw
caste – a subdivision of religion

(2) corps – military unit
corps – a dead body

(3) descent – get down
decent – good mannered

(4) die – lose life
dye – colour

(5) meat - flesh
meet – see each other

(6) tail – hindermost part of the body which long like a cord
tale – story

(7) weak - fragile
week – a group of seven days

(8) seem – appear
seam – a junction of line in between two pieces of cloth

EXERCISE

Q: Write down ten pairs of words having similar pronunciation but different meanings.

(1)	(6)
(2)	(7)
(3)	(8)
(4)	(9)
(5)	(10)

Chapter-19

Accent is the pitch in speaking. A good dictionary shows where the accent of each word is located. It is marked by "'" immediately after the syllable that carries the main stress such as:

ber'ry	grav'ity
blis'ter	gro'cer
burs'ar	han'dle
civ'ic	her'oin
cord'ial	in'come
corr'elate	i'ron
cour'age	lan'guage
cy'press	lo'tus
dan'ger	med'itate
daz'zle	mo'bile
de'cent	mu'tual
decep'tion	off'ice
dul'cet	ox'ygen
dumm'y	pi'lot
ed'ucate	ra'pid
ena'ble	rhet'oric
equiv'alent	sta'bilize
fiss'ure	sten'cil
flow'er	tar'tar
for'est	ti'tle
for'feit	ver'y
grad'uate	wat'er

EXERCISE

Q. Rewrite the following words marking accent.
centimetre, confide, democracy, expedient, faction, flora, gregarious, grocer, incorporate, ladder, marina, mammoth, microwave, overtime, outlook, pillar, poodle, plenty, proxy, punctual, raring, relation, reservoir, saddle, savage, setter, sewage, shallow, sherry, slumber, specimen, stagnate, subsidiary, subway, tentative, trachea, vermin

Ans:

Chapter-20

Ordinary dictionaries give meanings of English terms. But good dictionaries give not only the meanings of English terms but also foreign terms. As these foreign terms found their way into English vocabulary, they should also be part of a dictionary. So good dictionaries contain such terms. Some of them are given below. Try to find them in your dictionary.

bonafide	—	in good faith
bonvoyage	—	wish a good journey
en bloc	—	as a single unit
ex gratia	—	an act of grace
infra	—	below
lingua franca	—	common language
nom de plume	—	pen name
par excellence	—	eminently
sub Rosa	—	privately
supra	—	above
ultra vires	—	beyond one's power
via media	—	a middle way
vox populi	—	the voice of the people
ibidem	—	in the same place
post script	—	written after
incognito	—	unknown

EXERCISE

Q. Write down some foreign terms and their meaning that you could find in your dictionary.

Ans:

Chapter-21

A large number of abbreviated forms are in daily use. As they constitute a very large portion of English vocabulary, they cannot be ignored. Good dictionaries contain important abbreviations. Check if the following abbreviations are there in your dictionary.

LED	—	light-emitting diode
EST	—	Eastern standard time
ESP	—	Extra sensory perception
NATO	—	North Atlantic Treaty Organisation
WHO	—	World Health Organisation
DJ	—	disc jockey
doz	—	dozen
Dr.	—	Doctor
GPO	—	General Post Office
kg	—	kilogram
PR	—	Public Relations
RA	—	Royal Academy
RU	—	Rugby Union
SS	—	Steam ship
STD	—	Subscriber Trunk Dialing
St.	—	Saint
TV	—	Television
UN	—	United Nations

EXERCISE

Q. Expand the following abbreviations

(a) INTELEX	(b) INTERPOL	(c) ITU
(d) BCG	(e) BTU	(f) BOAC
(g) ASLV	(h) AFL-CIO	(i) AC
(j) ADC	(k) SAARC	(l) GATT
(m) HQ		

Ans:

(a)	(b)	(c)
(d)	(e)	(f)
(g)	(h)	(i)
(j)	(k)	(l)
(m)		

Chapter-22

MISCELLANEOUS EXERCISES

1. Choose the group of letters which is not in alphabetical order.

(a) s, t, u, v (b) l, m, n, o (c) e, f, g, h (d) p, m, n, o

Ans:

2. Choose the group of words which is not in alphabetical order.

(a) attar, attitude, attribute, auction
(b) coupe, courage, course, cousin
(c) forenoon, forewarn, forehand, fret
(d) pond, raspberry, rate, recondition

Ans:

3. Rearrange the letters in each of the followings to get meaningful words.

(a) N A
(b) I S H
(c) A T B E L
(d) E N L I C P
(e) L E H I D
(f) N A D W
(g) N U R
(h) R A E H T

Ans:

(a)
(b)
(c)
(d)
(e)
(f)
(g)
(h)

4. Fill in the blanks with suitable letters to get meaningful words.

(a) a _ ter
(b) go _ l
(c) m _ ny
(d) mu _ t
(e) br _ _ e
(f) th _ _
(g) o _ _ e
(h) st _ _ y
(i) _ r
(j) s _ _

Ans:

(a)
(b)
(c)
(d)
(e)
(f)
(g)
(h)
(i)
(j)

5. Frame words using letters given in the first and second columns of the following table.

m n s b	oon	? ? ? ?

Ans:

m n s b	oon	------ ------ ------ ------

6. Find meanings of the following words.
(a) copy (b) direct
(c) house (d) order
(e) set

Ans:
(a)
(b)
(c)
(d)
(e)

7. Write noun, adjective, adverb and verb forms of he following words.

(a) sincere (b) condition (c) familiar (d) person
(e) success

Ans:

Word	Noun	Adjective	Adverb	Verb
sincere				
condition				
familiar				
person				
success				

8. Find suitable meanings from column B for the words given in column A.

A	B
club	rotation
eclipse	image carved on stone
revolve	covering
statue	association
mantle	blotting out of a heavenly body by another

Ans:

A	B
club	
eclipse	
revolve	
statue	
mentle	

9. Read the following passage and pick out noun, adjectives, adverbs and verbs from it.

Christianity has been obsessed with satanic possession from earliest times. If Jesus was indeed the son of God it is strange that he failed to see possession was nothing but mental disease. But he went about casting out devils, and church officials followed his example exorcising victims who would be treated today in psychiatric clinics. The spiritual stature of a catholic priest depended on the number of imps he got out of a victim. This he did by branding, Thrashing and abusing the person with the vilest epithets- not unlike our own tantriks, satan was supposedly frightened of big words, so Greek and Latin was strung together to thunder at him. Other remedies were similar to ours- burning rank – smelling sulphur, smearing urine and fecal matter.

(Indian Skeptic 15-9-1999)

Ans:

Noun	Verb	Adjective	Adverb

10. Give the five examples for accent.

Ans: (a) (b)

(c) (d)

(e)

11. Give five words each for having the following prefixes.

(a) anti (b) a (c) dis

Ans:

(a)	(b)	(c)
1.	1.	1.
2.	2.	2.
3.	3.	3.
4.	4.	4.
5.	5.	5.

12. Give three words each for having the following suffixes.

(a) –er (b) –ist (c) –ice (d) –hood

Ans:

(a)	(b)	(c)	(d)
1.	1.	1.	1.
2.	2.	2.	2.
3.	3.	3.	3.

13. Write pronunciation of the following words in your vernacular language.

1. prepared 6. measure
2. card 7. plankton
3. board 8. psychiatrist
4. chivalry 9. critic
5. knives 10. physics

Ans: (1) (6)

(2) (7)

(3) (8)

(4) (9)

(5) (10)

14. Write five examples for homophones.

Ans: (1) (2) (3)

(6) (5)

15. Write five examples for homonyms.

Ans: (1) (2) (3)

(4) (5)

16. Give meaning:

(a) Aide de camp (b) Ex parte
(c) Status quo (d) vis-à-vis
(f) proforma

17. Expand the followings.

(a) GCC (b) FRCS (c) FIDE (d) EEC
(e) D.Sc.

Ans: (a)
(b)
(c)
(d)
(e)

18. Give antonyms of the followings.

(a) big (b) long (c) smile (d) cruel
(e) constant

Ans: (a) (b) (c) (d) (e)

19. Give synonyms of the followings.

(a) hard (b) imminent (c) queer (d) bliss
(e) remember

20. Note the difference between the words given in each pair given below.

(a) dear	(b) cheque	(c) course	(d) berth
deer	check	coarse	birth

Ans:

(a)

(b)

(c)

(d)

HOME STUDY SERIES - 1

SPELLING AND VOCABULARY

P. V. GOPALAKRISHNAN

SPELLING

CONTENTS

Sl. No.	Chapters	Exercise written date					Marks	Remarks
1.	The Letters							
2.	Spelling and Pronunciation							
3.	Spelling of some commonly used words							
4.	Plural formation							
5.	Homophones							
6.	Spelling rules							
7.	Past tense formation							
8.	Affixes							
9.	Special Spellings							
10.	Avoid confusion							
11.	Correct Spelling of some familiar names							
12.	Correct Spelling of some place names							
13.	Correct spelling of some familiar scientific terms							

1
The Letters

CAPITAL LETTERS OF ENGLISH

A B C D E F G H I J K L M N
O P Q R S T U V W X Y Z.

SMALL LETTERS OF ENGLISH

a b c d e f g h i j k l m n
o p q r s t u v w x y z

EXERCISES

I. Write capital letter forms of the following letters.

(a) q (b) t
(c) u (d) a

Ans: (a) __________ (b) __________
(c) __________ (d) __________

II. Write small letter forms of the following letters.

(a) R (b) E
(c) G (d) D
(e) M

Ans: (a) __________ (b) __________
(c) __________ (d) __________
(e) __________

III. Write all the capital letters of English.

Ans:

IV. Write all the small letters of English.

Ans:

2
Spelling and Pronunciation

English language is heterogeneous in nature. Hence spelling and pronunciation is distantly related. Go through the following letters(s). Note the difference in pronunciation when they come in different words.

Letter	A				
Pronunciation	अ	आ	एय	आय	ए
example word	at	arm	share	fare	way

Letter	B	
Pronunciation	ए (short)	ए (long)
example word	set	there

Letters	EW	
Pronunciation	इ	ऊ
example word	new	hew

Letter	I	
Pronunciation	ई	अ
example word	ill	first

Letters	Ee
Pronunciation	ई
example word	ill

Letters	Ea
Pronunciation	ई
example word	leach

EXERCISES

I. Write three words containing the letters 'A' having the pronunciation 'आ'

Ans: ____________ ____________ ____________

II. What is the pronunciation of 'a' in each of the following words.

(a) another (b) backward

(c) sat

Ans: (a) ____________ (b) ____________

(c) ____________

III. Give English equivalent for the followings.

(a) ई (b) एय

(c) ऊ (d) अ

Ans: (a) ____________ (b) ____________

(c) ____________ (c) ____________

IV. Write two words in which 'Ea' is pronounced as 'ई'

Ans: ____________ ____________

V. Give four words having different letters for the sound 'ई'

Ans: ____________ ____________

____________ ____________

Letters	o/oo			
Pronunciation	ओ	अ	उ	औ
example word	box	love	book	out

Letters	u		
Pronunciation	उ	यू	अ
example word	put	use	gun

Letters	y			
Pronunciation	इ	अय	ऐ	य
example word	policy	tyre	my	royal

B – ब (box)
C – क, स (cat, policy)
D – ड (dead)
F – फ (face)
G – ग (gain)
H – ह (hand)
J – ज (jail)
K – क (kill)
L – ल (load)
M – म (moon)
N – न (noon)
P – प (pain)
Q – क्यू (quick)
R – र (rail)
S – स (sail)
T – ट, ड्ड (train, till)

EXERCISES

I. Write Hindi equivalents of the underlined letters(s) in the following words.

(a) rice (b) reap
(c) post (d) port
(e) map (f) of
(g) too (h) big
(i) row

Ans: (a) ________ (b) ________
(c) ________ (d) ________
(e) ________ (f) ________
(g) ________ (h) ________
(i) ________

II. Write the pronunciation of the following words.

(a) preach (b) plan
(c) map (d) bid
(e) bat (f) up
(g) too (h) for

Ans: (a) ________ (b) ________
(c) ________ (d) ________
(e) ________ (f) ________

(g) ________ (h) ________

III. Write one example each in English for the following starting pronunciation.

(a) प (b) म

(c) ब (d) फ

(e) क (f) स

(g) र (h) ल

Ans: (a) ________ (b) ________

(c) ________ (d) ________

(e) ________ (f) ________

(g) ________ (h) ________

V – व

love

w – व

wood

z – ज़

zoo

kh – ख

lakhs

gh – घ, फ

Raghu, laugh

ch – च, ष

rich, chivalry

th – त

thin

dh – द

there

ph – फ

phone

sh – ष

shore

EXERCISES

I. What are the pronunciation of the following words. Write the pronunciation in Hindi. You may use a dictionary.

(a) progeny (b) villain
(c) ancient (d) kidnap
(e) blue (f) collar
(g) steal (h) angel
(i) their (j) son
(k) loose (l) jeep.

Ans: (a) ________ (b) ________
(c) ________ (d) ________
(e) ________ (f) ________
(g) ________ (h) ________
(i) ________ (j) ________
(k) ________ (l) ________

II. Write two words starting 'ज़' sound.

Ans: ____________ ____________

III. Write three words starting 'द'

Ans: ____________ ____________ ____________

IV. Write English equivalents for the underlined letter(s) in the following words.

(a) another (b) sea
(c) rice

Ans: (a) ________ (b) ________
(c) ________

3
Spelling of Some Commonly Used Words

I	had	so
me	this	out
my	these	to
we	those	on
us	that	too
our	here	up
you	there	how
our	a	what
he	an	where
him	the	when
his	at	whom
she	as	whose
her	on	which
it	in	do
its	my	does
they	of	did
them	for	can
their	off	may
are	with	will
am	yes	shall
is	no	could
was	be	should
were	bee	would
has	or	
have	and	

EXERCISES

I. Fill the blanks with the suitable spelling(s).

(a) do–s (b) wh–m

(c) –ad (d) ma–

(e) ther– (f) u–
(g) the– (h) u–on

Ans: (a) ________ (b) ________
(c) ________ (d) ________
(e) ________ (f) ________
(g) ________ (h) ________

II. Re-write the letters of words given below to get meaningful words.

(a) houlds (b) os
(c) ehtre (d) ta
(e) ish (f) ouyr
(g) ihs (h) od.

Ans: (a) ________ (b) ________
(c) ________ (d) ________
(e) ________ (f) ________
(g) ________ (h) ________

III. Supply with the missed letter(s)

(a) culd (b) ther
(c) whos (d) wer

Ans: (a) ________ (b) ________
(c) ________ (d) ________

IV. Write in English

(a) युवर (b) वास
(c) हि (d) मै

Ans: (a) ________ (b) ________
(c) ________ (d) ________

4
Plural Formation

Plurals of a large number of English nouns are formed by adding the letter 's' to the hindermost part of the noun.

E.g: Pen - Pens
Pencil - Pencils

But in the case of words ending in -s, -sh, -ch, -z, -x, 'es' should be added to the noun for making its plural.

E.g: box - boxes
glass - glasses

Nouns ending in '-y' preceded by a consonant should be suffixed by '-ies' after omitting 'y'. At the same time one thing should be remembered that final 'y' which do not proceded by a consonant need not be replaced.

E.g: baby - babies
toy - toys
city - cities
boy - boys

Final 'f/fe' of singular nouns is changed by 'ves' for forming their plurals.

E.g: knife - knives
calf - calves

SPELLING STUDY

abbreviate, accommodate, achieve, acquiesce, across, address, affection, agreeable, already, analyse, ancient, angle, anomaly, anxiety, appearance, ascent, avaricious.

EXERCISES

I. Write plurals of the following nouns.

(a) toy (b) monkey
(c) story

Ans: (a) ________ (b) ________
(c) ________

II. Rewrite the followings if incorrect.

(a) afection (b) achieve
(c) abreviate (d) anxity
(e) ancient (f) agreeble.

Ans: (a) ________ (b) ________
(c) ________ (d) ________
(e) ________ (f) ________

III. Supply with the missed letter(s).

(a) Du– (b) d–spose
(c) glanc– (d) jealo–s
(e) k—n (f) of–ice.

Ans: (a) ________ (b) ________
(c) ________ (d) ________
(e) ________ (f) ________

IV. What are the spelling rules of plural formation?

Ans:

5
Homo Phones-1

Note the difference in spelling of words in each pair given below though they are pronounced similarly.

(1) almost
all most
(2) already
all ready
(3) ascent
assent
(4) ascetic
acetic
(5) alms
arms
(6) advice
advise
(7) bail
bale
(8) ballad
ballade
(9) banquet
banquette
(10) beet
beat
(11) beach
beech
(12) berth
birth
(13) bloc
block
(14) blond
blonde
(15) born
borne
(16) bough
bow
(17) breach
breech
(18) bread
bred
(19) bridal
bridle
(20) buoy
boy

SPELLING STUDY

awkward, balloon, because, bicycle, biscuit, brake, budget, business, carrying, caught, character, coarse, commemorate.

EXERCISES

I. Write pronounciation and meaning of the words in each pair given below. You may use a dictionary

(a) bloc
block
(b) beet
beat
(c) alms
arms
(d) ballad
ballade

(e) buoy
boy

Ans: (a) (b)
(c) (d)
(e)

II. Correct the spelling

(a) bicicle (b) carring
(c) busines (d) brack
(e) corse (f) comemorate

Ans: (a) ________ (b) ________
(c) ________ (d) ________
(e) ________ (f) ________

III. What is the difference between 'bail' and bale.

Ans:

Homo Phones – 2

(1) cannon
canon
(2) caste
cast
(3) callous
callus
(4) canvas
canvass
(5) carat
carot
(6) cereal
serial
(7) cease
seize
(8) cheque
check
(9) cite
site
(10) coma
comma
(11) complement
compliment
(12) confident
confidant
(13) cord
chord
(14) corps
corpse
(15) cost
coast
(16) counsel
council
(17) councilor
counselor
(18) course
coarse
(19) creak
creek
(20) currant
current
(21) diary
dairy
(22) decease
disease
(23) decree
degree
(24) dear
deer.

SPELLING STUDY

Committee, conceit, conceive, conscience, condemn, deceive, development, dexterous, disease, dyeing, eccentric, embarrass, emphasize, exaggerate, excellent, exhaust.

EXERCISES

I. Write pronunciation and meaning of the words in each pair given below. You may use a dictionary.

(a) cost
coast

(b) dear
deer

(c) coma
comma

(d) cord
chord

Ans: (a)
(b).
(c)
(d)

II. Supply with suitable spelling(s)

(a) conc_ _ve
(b) embar_ass
(c) conce_t
(d) dise_se
(e) dy_ing
(f) excel_ent

Ans: (a) ________
(b) ________
(c) ________
(d) ________
(e) ________
(f) ________

III. Correct the spelling.

(a) emphasise
(b) commitee
(c) developement

Ans:

Homophones – 3

(1) descent
decent

(2) desert
dessert

(3) device
devise

(4) die
dye

(5) discuss
discus

(6) dose
doze

(7) divers
diverse

(8) dual
duel

(9) draught
drought

(10) earn
yearn

(11) fare
fair
(12) flair
flare
(13) flea
flee
(14) flour
flower
(15) foul
fowl
(16) freize
freeze
(17) gait
gate
(18) gild
guild
(19) gorilla
guerrilla
(20) grand
grant

SPELLING STUDY

exercise, extreme, favourite, foreign, forty, freight, gauge, goal, government, grief, guard, heal, heart, hideous, humour, hypocrisy, immediately, impostor.

EXERCISES

I. Write pronunciation and meaning of the words in each pair given below. You may use a dictionary.

(a) die
dye
(b) foul
fowl
(c) grand
grant
(d) desert
dessert

Ans: (a) (b)
(c) (d)

II. Correct the spelling

(a) guirrilla (b) heer
(c) lessan (d) immedietely
(e) extrem

Ans: (a) ________ (b) ________
(c) ________ (d) ________
(e) ________

III. Supply with appropriate spelling.

(a) fore_gn (b) gri_f
(c) humo_r

Ans: (a) ________ (b) ________
(c) ________

Homophones-4 (cont.)

(1) heal
heel
(2) hear
here
(3) heard
herd
(4) heu
hew
(5) later
latter
(6) lathe
lath
(7) lead
led
(8) lessen
lesson
(9) liver
lever
(10) lose
loose
(11) male
mail
(12) miner
minor
(13) meat
meet
(14) mean
meen
(15) modal
model
(16) mucous
mucus
(17) naval
navel
(18) passed
past
(19) personal
personnel
(20) practice
practise
(21) pray
prey
(22) precedent
president

SPELLING STUDY

incite, inquire, inventor, jealous, jeweller, journey, kaleidoscope, kindergarten, knave, kneel, knife, knowledge, labour, league, leisure, lettuce, licence, lieutenant.

EXCERCISES

I. Write pronunciation and meaning of the words in each pair given below. You may use a dictionary.

(a) prey
pray

(b) modal
model

(c) heu
hew

(d) hear
here

Ans: (a)

(b)

(c)

(d)

II. Correct the followings.

(a) labur

(b) jeweler

(c) inquire (d) letuce
(e) liutenant (f) knil

Ans: (a) ________ (b) ________
(b) ________ (d) ________
(e) ________ (f) ________

III. Supply with suitable spelling(s).

(a) kindergar-en (b) -nowledge
(c) li-ence (d) kal_idoscope.

Ans: (a) ________ (b) ________
(c) ________ (d) ________

Homophones-5 (cont.)

(1) patrol
petrol
(2) plain
plane
(3) price
prize
(4) queue
cue
(5) role
roll
(6) sale
sail
(7) seam
seem
(8) soar
sore
(9) sole
soul
(10) scene
seen
(11) storey
story
(12) straight
strait
(13) stile
style
(14) suit
suite
(15) sweet
sweat
(16) stationary
stationery
(17) steel
steal
(18) tale
tail
(19) team
teem
(20) therefore
therefor
(21) tire
tyre
(22) to
too
(23) waste
waist
(24) waive
wave
(25) weak
week

SPELLING STUDY

loose, lovable, manoeuvre, massacre, meant, mileage, missionary, movable, mysterious, niece, novice, nuisance, obvious, occurred, opposite, parliament, pedlar, persuit, phantom

EXCERCISES

I. Write pronunciation and meaning of the words in each pair given below.

(a) stile
style

(b) team
teem

(c) sale
sail

(d) plain
plane

Ans: (a) (b)
(c) (d)

II. Supply with suitable spelling(s)

(a) mysteri_us
(b) mov_ble
(c) lo_se
(d) nuis_nce
(e) mis_ionary

Ans: (a) __________ (b) __________
(c) __________ (d) __________
(e) __________

III. Correct the spelling

(a) obvious
(b) meent
(c) manuvre
(d) oposite
(e) ocurred
(f) pedler

Ans: (a) __________ (b) __________
(c) __________ (d) __________
(e) __________ (f) __________

6
Spelling Rules

DOUBLING

Final consonant of a word doubles on adding a suffix which starts with a vowel, if it is preceded by a single vowel.

E.g: rub + ed → rubbed
get + ing → getting

FINAL 'e'

Final 'e' of words is dropped before adding a suffix that start with a vowel, if the 'e' is preceded by at least one consonant.

E.g: waste + ing → wasting
live + ing → living

'l' in all/full

Final 'l' of 'all' and 'full' is dropped when they are added to a word as prefix and suffix respectively.

E.g: all + ready → already
all + together → altogether
cheer + full → cheerful
thank + full → thankful

SPELLING STUDY

picturesque, pigeon, pleasure, possess, practice, precede, privilege, progeny, proof, pursuit, quick, queue, receive, religion, rhyme, rogue, scene, scissors.

EXERCISES

I. Supply with suitable spelling(s).

(a) pursu_t (b) practic_
(c) pig_on (d) po_ _es_
(e) sci_sors

Ans: (a) ________ (b) ________
(c) ________ (d) ________
(e) ________

II. Combine.

(a) mouth + full (b) all + right

Ans: (a) ________ (b) ________

III. When the final 'e' of a word is dropped? Give two examples.

Ans:

IV. Briefly describe the doubling rules. Give examples.

7

Past Tense Information

Past tense form of a regular verb is made by suffixing '_d/_ed' to its present tense form.

E.g: work + ed → worked
receive + d → received
Final 'y' of words ending in 'y' preceded by a vowel is changed to 'i' and suffixed with 'd' to form its past.

E.g: pay → paid
lay → laid
In some other cases final 'd' is changed to 't' to form past form.

E.g: send → sent
words ending in -s, -sh, -ch, -z, -x should be suffixed with 'ed' to form past form. Past tense form of some words are the very same form of the present tense itself.

E.g: put → put
cut → cut

SPELLING STUDY

secretary, seize, sergeant, shoes, seige, solemn, sincerely, sovereign stirred, subtlety, suicide, sulphur, summary, symmetry, tense, throne, through, transferred, treacherous.

EXERCISES

I. Write past form of the following present tenses. You may use a dictionary or a grammar book.

(a) prepare (b) come
(c) wash (d) deceive

II. Correct the spelling.

(a) soverein (b) suiside
(c) shoos (d) solem
(e) tence

Ans: (a) ________ (b) ________
(c) ________ (d) ________
(e) ________

III. Supply with suitable spelling(s).

(a) sum_ary (b) treacher_ _s

(c) sei_e (d) sin_ _rely

Ans: (a) ________ (b) ________

(c) ________ (d) ________

IV. What are the rules of past tense formation?

Ans:

8
Affixes

(1)-age

When the suffix word '-age' is added to a word ending in 'e', the final 'e' is normally dropped.

E.g: line + age → linage

(2) Final 'c'

Final 'c' of most of the words has a 'k' sound. Hence when suffixes like -er, -ed, -ing, -y etc are added to a word 'k' is also inserted to get the sound of 'k'.

E.g: zinc + y → zincky.

(3) Final 'd'

final 'd' of the word 'bed' is doubled when a suffix having a vowel starting is added to it.

E.g: bed + ing → bedding.

'y' is added to words ending in '-ie' before suffixing 'ing'.

E.g: die + ing → dying

lie + ing → lying

In such cases, the final 'e' is dropped.

SPELLING STUDY

undue, university, utterance, vacuum, valley, valour, veterinary, villain, volleys, volunteer, wagon, wednesday, wholly, woe, woollen, writ, yacht, zero, zoo.

EXERCISES

I. Correct the spelling

(a) veterinery (b) vollies

(c) valor (d) yaat

(e) wensday (f) voluntier

Ans: (a) ________ (b) ________

(c) ________ (d) ________

(e) ________ (f) ________

II. When should the letter 'k' be added to the final 'c' of some words. Give three examples.

Ans:

III. Use a dictionary and find some words having an '-age' suffix.

9

Special Spellings

DOUBLE 's'

assassin, assault, assemble, assent, asset, assign, assist, associate, assume.

DOUBLE 't'

attach, attack, attempt, attend, attest, attract, attribute

DOUBLE 'r'

arrange, array, arrears, arrest, arrive, arrow.

DOUBLE 'p'

apparatus, apparent, appeal, append, appendix, apply, appoint, appreciate, approach, appropriate, approve, approxiamately.

DOUBLE 'l'

allergy, alley, allow, allude, allot.

DOUBLE 'f'

affect, affection, affirm, affix, afford, affray

EXERCISES

I. Correct the spelling.

(a) asist (b) apoint
(c) alude (d) afirm
(e) apendex (f) ariers
(g) arang (h) asent

Ans: (a) ________ (b) ________
(c) ________ (d) ________
(e) ________ (f) ________
(g) ________ (h) ________

II. Use a dictionary and find any five words having double 'r', other than given above

Ans: ________ ________ ________
________ ________

III. Write six words, otherthan given in the last page, having double 'p'. You may use a dictionary.

Ans: ________ ________ ________

________ ________ ________

IV. Write six words, other than given in the last page, having double 'l'. You may use a dictionary.

Ans: ________ ________ ________

________ ________ ________

10
Avoid Confusion

(1) aught/ought

aught	ought
caught	bought
taught	brought
	fought
	ought
	sought
	thought

(2) ary/ery/ory

ary	ery	ory
adversary	confectionery	aditory
commentary	millinery	circulatory
complementary	stationery	contributory
secondary		migratory
secretary		promissory
temporary		signatory
		transitory

(3) anti/ante

anti	ante
antibiotic	antechamber
antibody	antemeridian
antiseptic	anteroom
antisocialist	

EXERCISES

I. Use a dictionary and write down all the words suffixed with 'aught' and 'ought' that you can find.

Ans:

II. Correct the spelling.
(a) millianary (b) promissery

(c) secretery

Ans: (a) ________ (b) ________

(c) ________

III. What is the difference between 'anti' and 'ante'? Give two examples for each.

Ans:

IV. Find some words from your dictionary that have 'ery' ending. Arrange them below in the alphabetical order.

Ans:

Avoid confusion (cont.)

(1) able/ible

able	ible
adorable	accessible
agreeable	admissible
amiable	comprehensible
arguable	credible
believable	divisible
blamable	edible
changeable	eligible
comfortable	expressible
debatable	feasible
drinkable	flexible
eatable	forcible
forgettable	gullible
forgivable	incredible
immovable	indefeasible
inprovable	indigestible
incurable	inflexible
inestimable	intelligible
inflatable	irressitible
likable	legible
lovable	negligible

EXERCISES

I. Use a dictionary and find some words which have 'able' and 'ible' endings.

Ans:

able	ible

Avoid confusion (cont.)

(1) able/ible

able	ible
movable	ostensible
notable	perceptible
peaceable	personable
persuasible	probable
retucible	provable
responsible	reasonable
reversible	removable
submersible	serviceable
suppressible	teachable
susceptible	tolerable
tangible	treasonable
transmissible	ungovernable
vendible	unmistakable
visible	unquenchable
unshakable	

EXERCISES

I. Use a dictionary and find some words which have 'able' and 'ible' endings.

Ans:

able	ible

11
Correct Spelling of Some Familiar Names

Aeschylus
Albert Einstein
Aldous Huxley
Alexandre Dumas
Aristotle
Auden
Beethoven
Carl Gustav Jung
Dante
Destoievsky
Euripides
Guy de Maupassant
Heinmann
Henrik Ibsen
Herodotus
Ibanez
Jean Paul
Jesperson
John Galsworthy
Knut Hamsen
Krushchev
Leonardo Da Vinci
Malthus
Maxim Gorky
Moliere
Nitzche
Oedipus
Paul Julius Reuter
Picaso
Romain Rolland
Sainte Beuve
Schiller
Sigmund Freud
Somerset Maugham
Soren Kierkegaard
Turgenev
Van Gogh
Washington Irving

EXERCISES

I. Correct the spelling .

(a) Aristotil (b) Yung
(c) Ebsen (d) Edipus
(e) Maum (f) Oden

Ans: (a) ________ (b) ________
(c) ________ (d) ________
(e) ________ (f) ________

II. Write down for your record all the other names whose spelling confuse you.

12
Correct Spelling of Some Place Names

Beijing
Boston
Cairo
Cambridge
Chennai
Chicago
Delhi
Dover
Hong Kong
Honolulu
Istanbul
Johannesburg
Logos
London
Los Angeles
Mexico City
Miami
Montreal
Moscow
Mumbai
Nairobi
New Orleans
New York
Oxford
Paris
Perth
Rome
San Francisco
Santiago
Sydney
Tokyo
Vienna
Washington

EXERCISES

I. Correct the spelling.

(a) Johanesberg (b) Londen
(c) Tokiyo (d) Chikago
(e) Beejing (f) Mosko

Ans: (a) ________ (b) ________
(c) ________ (d) ________
(e) ________ (f) ________

II. Write down for your record the names of places whose spelling confuse you.

Ans:

13
Correct Spelling of Some Familiar Scientific Terms

acceleration
adventitious
aerial
albumen
alga
algebra
alimentary canal
allotrope
alloy
amoeba
amphibious
amplifier
analogy
anode
antenna
anthropology
antisymmetric
aqueous
artery
assimilation
astigmatism
asymmetry
axiom
bacillus
bacteria
barometer
binomial
buoyancy
buttress root
catalysis
cathode
centrifugal
chlorophyll
chromosome
coagulate
coefficient
coherent
coluomb
compression
condenser
configuration
congruent
corollary
corrosion
crystallisation
curvature
cyst

EXERCISES

I. Correct the spelling.

(a) klorophil
(b) korolery
(c) sist
(d) basillus
(e) ameeba
(f) kathod.

Ans: (a)
(b)
(c)
(d)
(e)
(f)

II. Write down other scientific terms whose spelling confuse you.

Ans:

Correct spelling of some familiar scientific terms (cont.)

decay
deviation
diaphram
diffraction
dispersion
distillation
divergence
eccentricity
ecology
electrode
ellipse
embryo
emission
emulsion
endosperm
epidermis
equilibrium
evaporation
extinction
fermentation
fertilization
fission
fluorescence
fossil
fraction
gall bladder
graph
herbaceous
hermaphrodite
heterogeneous
hexagonal
homogeneous
hybridization
hypothetical
incandescent
incombustible
inert
inflammable
interference
inversion
isolated
isotope
kidney
kinetic

EXERCISES

I. Correct the spelling.

(a) icology (b) fosil
(c) fluresent (d) fishion
(e) homogenus (f) herbacins

Ans: (a) (b)
(c) (d)
(e) (f)

II. Write down other scientific terms whose spelling confuse you.

Ans:

Correct spelling of some familiar scientific terms (cont.)

latitude	overtone
lemma	oxidation
longitude	parallel
lubrication	parasite
lymph	penumbra
magnetism	pericardium
mammal	pericycle
mass	permeability
membrane	perpendicular
metallurgy	pivot
microscope	placenta
molecule	plankton
monochromatic	polarisation
monocotyledon	polygon
multiplicity	pressure
mutation	prism
node	propagation
nucleus	qualitative
octahedron	quantitative
orthogonal	quantum
orthorhombic	resonance
oscillation	solubility
osmosis	solvent

EXERCISES

I. Correct the spelling.

(a) peri kardium (b) plasenta
(c) kuantom (d) mas
(e) mikcroskope (f) parelel

Ans: (a) (b)
(c) (d)
(e) (f)

II. Write down other scientific terms whose spelling confuse you.

Ans:

VOCABULARY

CONTENTS

SL. NO.	CHAPTERS	EXCERCISE WRITTENDATE						RE-WRIT-TENDATE	MARKS	REMARKS
		I	II	III	IV	V	VI			
1.	Course-1									
2.	Course-2									
3.	Course-3									
4.	Course-4									
5.	Course-5									
6.	Course-6									
7.	Course-7									
8.	Course-8									
9.	Course-9									
10.	Course-10									
11.	Course-11									
12.	Course-12									
13.	Course-13									
14.	Course-14									
15.	Course-15									
16.	Course-16									
17.	Course-17									
18.	Course-18									
19.	Course-19									

SL. NO.	CHAPTERS	EXCERCISE WRITTENDATE						RE-WRIT-TENDATE	MARKS	REMARKS
		I	II	III	IV	V	VI			
20.	Course-20									
21.	Course-21									
22.	Course-22									
23.	Course-23									
24.	Course-24									
25.	Course-25									
26.	Course-26									

Course – 1

1. **Meaning**

abbrevaite	– shorten	agree	– comply
ability	– capacity	aid	– help
abnormal	– irregular	alarm	– warning
above	– over	allow	– permit
absent	– not present	alter	– change
accept	– take	altogether	– completely
ache	– pain	ambition	– desire
achieve	– win	amid	– in the middle
add	– include	ancient	– old
adequate	– enough	apply	– request
admire	– showing respect	appreciate	– enjoy
adult	– grown up	approach	– near
affectionate	– loving	approve	– permit
affix	– add	argue	– disagree

2. **opposite**

above × below
accept × reject
agree × differ
ancient × modern
arrive × depart
attract × repel

3. **Ask your parent**

I	it	her	me	their
you	my	its	him	us
he	your	we	our	them
she	his	they		

EXERCISES

I. Give one word for the following ideas.
(a) not present.
(b) something irregular.

Ans: (a) ____________ (b) ____________

II. Find the other meanings of the following words. You may use a dictionary.
(a) appreciate (b) adequate

Ans: (a) ____________ (b) ____________

III. Find the opposites of the following words. You may use a thesaurus.

(a) ancient (b) artificial

Ans: (a) (b)

IV. Use in sentence.

(a) our (b) his

Ans: (a)

(b)

Course - 2

1. **Meaning**

arrest	– check	beneath	– under
artificial	– unreal	beside	– near
assassinate	– political killing	bit	– very small piece
attempt	– venture	blame	– accuse
author	– writer	bliss	– pleasure
avoid	– keep away	bold	– courageous
back	– support	brave	– courageous
balance	– remainder	breath	– intake of air
before	– in front of	bring	– take to near
begin	– start		

2. **Opposite**

beautiful × ugly
belief × doubt
bright × dim
cheap × costly
clean × dirty
common × rare
dark × light
deep × shallow
exit × entrance
external × internal
famous × obscure
fat × lean
foreign × native
full × empty
gain × loss
general × special
guilty × innocent
hate × love
heavy × light
high × low
honour × shame
host × guest

3. **Ask your parent**
am, is, are, was, were, have, has, had, do, does, did, shall, will, would, can, could, may, might, must, ought to, need, used to.

EXERCISES

I. Use the following words in sentence.
(a) will (b) were
(c) do

Ans: (a) (b)
(c)

II. Write any five words and their meanings which come between 'bliss' and 'brave' in your dictionary.

Ans: (1) __________ : ____________________

(2) __________ : ____________________

(3) __________ : ____________________

(4) __________ : ____________________

(5) __________ : ____________________

III. Give opposites of the following words.

(a) brave (b) beside

(c) low (d) hate

(e) loss

Ans: (a)__________ (b) __________

(c) __________ (d) __________

(e) __________

IV. Give one words for the following ideas.

(a) One who writes books.

(b) One who kills for money or political reasons.

Ans: (a)

(b)

Course- 3

1. **Meaning**

cabin	– small room	collapse	– break away
calamity	– disaster	collect	– gather
calculate	– count	command	– order
calm	– mild	commence	– start
cancel	– ignore	compel	– force
cardinal	– principal	complete	– full
cashier	– cash dealer	compute	– calculate
casual	– unexpected	conceal	– hide
catastrophe	– mishap	concise	– brief
centre	– middle part	confidential	– secret
chance	– opportunity	consent	– agree
chapter	– lesson	conserve	– preserve
charity	– kindness	construct	– build
cheap	– low	contaminate	– make bad
chief	– main	cordial	– hearty
choose	– select		

2. **Opposite**

hurt × heal	joy × sorrow
idle × busy	kind × cruel
import × export	later × earlier
inferior × superior	lead × follow
input × output	lend × borrow

3. **Ask your parent**
to, by, with, in, at, between, among, on, at, below, into, upon, within, since, for, up, towards, of, across, behind, about, above.

EXERCISES

I. Use in sentence.

(a) among (b) upon
(c) on (d) at

Ans: (a) (b)
(c) (d)

II. Find the other meanings of the following words. You may use a dictionary.

(a) chief (b) calm

(c) concise (d) compute

Ans: (a) (b)

(c) (d)

III. Write the opposite of the following words.

(a) consent (b) cheap

(c) build (d) conceal

(e) collect

Ans: (a) (b)

(c) (d)

(e)

Course – 4

1. **Meaning**

debate	– argue	disciple	– pupil
deed	– act	disclose	– reveal
deficient	– insufficient	disgust	– hatred
delight	– pleasure	despatch	– send
den	– cave	disperse	– scatter
denote	– point	dispute	– argue
depression	– sorrow	distant	– far away
describe	– explain	disturb	– trouble
destiny	– fate	doctrine	– principle
determine	– decide	drug	– medicine

2. **Opposite**

loose × tight	rapid × slow
many × few	remember × forget
motion × rest	retail × whole sale
natural × artificial	rise × fall
negative × positive	safe × risky
odd × even	simple × complex
offer × refuse	smile × frown
oral × written	solid × liquid
permit × prohibit	strange × familiar
praise × blame	succeed × fail
profit × loss	sure × doubtful
public × private	

3. **Ask your parent**

statue, prisoner, municipality, panchayat, queen, king, governor, infantry, artillery, revenue, ancient, baron, rebellion, ruler, conqueror, reformation, renaissance, cabinet.

EXERCISES

I. Use in sentence.

(a) ruler (b) king

(c) panchayat (d) prisoner.

Ans: (a)

(b)

(c)

(d)

II. Write three opposites each of the following words. You may use a thesaurus.

(a) oral (b) rise

(c) rapid (d) permit

(e) motion

Ans: (a) ____________ ____________ ____________

(b) ____________ ____________ ____________

(c) ____________ ____________ ____________

(d) ____________ ____________ ____________

(e) ____________ ____________ ____________

III. Write three more meanings for each of the following words. You may use a dictionary.

(a) disturb (b) delight

Ans: (a) ____________ ____________ ____________

(b) ____________ ____________ ____________

Course - 5

1. Meaning

edge	– border	eradicate	– root out
edible	– eatable	erect	– vertical
effect	– result	err	– mistake
efficient	– able	esteem	– respect
eligible	– deserving	event	– incident
embarrass	– perplex	exact	– correct
emblem	– symbol	except	-- exclude
enhance	– increase	expend	– spend
enourmous	– huge	explain	– describe
ensure	– make sure	external	– outer.
entire	– full		

2. Opposite

sweet × bitter
tall × short
thick × thin
top × bottom
triumph × defeat
true × false
upper × lower
urban × rural
vague × clear
vertical × horizontal
victory × defeat
virtue × vice
wake × sleep
wealth × poverty
wide × narrow
win × lose
wise × foolish.

3. Ask your parent

artic, antarctic, amazon, pacific, solar, lunar, erosion, weathering, peninsular, plateau, plain, orbit, delta, valley, hemisphere, horizon, latitude, longitude, population, continent, island, communication.

EXERCISES

I. Use a dictionary and find all the antonyms of the following words.

(a) entire (b) exact
(c) explain (d) esteem

Ans: (a)

(b)

(c)

(d)

II. Find the opposites of the following words using a thesaurus.

(a) victory (b) wide

(c) rural (d) thin

(e) wise

Ans: (a)

(b)

(c)

(d)

(e)

III. Use in sentence.

(a) pacific (b) delta

(c) island

Ans: (a)

(b)

(c)

Course- 6

1. Meaning

fact	– real data	flair	– inborn talent
faint	– weak	flimsy	– thin
fair	– beautiful	force	– power
fate	– destiny	forgive	– pardon
fault	– mistake	format	– model
feeble	– weak	fortune	– luck
feel	– experience	forward	– preface
festival	– celebration	fraud	– deceit
fine	– very good	fundamental	– basic

2. Foreign words

agenda	– matters to be done	pari passu	– with the same force
bonafide	– in good faith		
en route	– on the way	per capita	– per head
in camera	– in secret	post mortem	– after death
in toto	– entirely	versus	– against
ipso facto	– automatically	vis-a-vis	– opposite

3. Ask your parent

second, minute, hour, day, week, month, year, decade, century, day-night, age, morning, evening, midnight, moment, afternoon, noon, forenoon.

EXERCISES

I. Use in sentence.

(a) age (b) hour

(c) morning (d) noon

Ans: (a)

(b)

(c)

(d)

II. Use the following foreign terms in sentence.
(a) ipso facto (b) versus

Ans: (a)

(b)

III. Write any five words and their meanings, which come between 'format' and 'fraud'. You may use a dictionary.

Ans: (a)

(b)

(c)

(d)

(e)

Course-7

1. **meaning**

gather	–	collect	grant	–	permit
general	–	public	grateful	–	thankful
ghost	–	spirit	grief	–	sorrow
glad	–	happy	grow	–	increase
goal	–	aim	guard	–	protector
gossip	–	rumour	guy	–	young fellow
grand	–	great			

2. **Idioms**

come around	—	refrain from
make out	—	understand
do away with	—	abolish
by hook or crook	—	by any means
play fast and loose	—	flexible character
in the long run	—	in the end
keep pace with	—	regular progress
get into hot water	—	get troubled
in high spirits	—	cheerful
spread like wild fire	—	rapid spreading
take to heels	—	run
on all fours	—	similar
bad blood	—	intentionally

3. **Ask your parent**

Sunday, Monday, Tuesday, Wedesday, Thursday, Friday, Saturday, iron, marble, tin, steel, copper, bronze, coal, chalk, silver, zinc, sulphur

EXCERCISES

I. Use the following idioms in sentence.

(a) take to heels (b) by hook or crook

(c) make out

An: (a)

(b)

(c)

II. Which day comes after Friday?

An:

III. Use in sentence.

(a) Tuesday (b) coal

An: (a)

(b)

IV. Write two synonyms of the following words. You may use a dictionary.

(a) grief (b) grand

(c) general (d) gather

An: (a)

(b)

(c)

(d)

Course-8

1. **Meaning**

halt – stop		heal – cure	
handsome – beautiful		hit – strike	
harm – hurt		homage – respect	
harmony – agreement		hue – colour	
hay – drygrass		huge – very big	
		hypocrisy – pretence	

2. **Idioms**

out of the question—impossible
in full swing—very active
a mare's nest—worthless thing
cook the accounts—make false accounts
spur of the moment—without thinking
blow one's own trumpet—boast
come to grief—fail
black sheep—bad characters
once in a blue moon—rarely
quisling—a traitor
bed of roses—confortable condition
bed of thorns—uncomfortable condition

3. **Ask your parent**

axis, circle, mathematics, algebra, formulae, decimal, arithmetic, metre, geometry, coincide, radius, corresponding diameter, equal, division, sustraction, multiply, triangle, equilibrium, horizontal, equation, percentage, hexagon, quarter, ratio.

EXCERCISES

I. Use in sentence.
(a) decimal (b) square
(c) coincide.

An: (a)

(b)

(c)

II. Write two synonyms each of the following words. You may use a dictionary.

(a) heal (b) hue

(c) harm

An: (a) ________ ________

(b) ________ ________

(c) ________ ________

III. Use in sentence.

(a) once in a blue moon (b) come to grief

An: (a)

(b)

Course-9

1. **Meaning**

ignorance—unawareness
immediate—sudden
immortal—eternal
impact—influence
impede—hindrance
implore—request
improve—make better
imprudent—rash
incompetent—unskilled
inconsistent—changeable
indeed—truly
independent—free
inevitable—unavoidable
infamous—notorious
ingratitude—thankless
innumerable—countless
insignificant—silly
instance—example
instruct—teach
interview—meeting
intimate—close
invade—attack
irrational—unreasoable
isolate—separate.

2. **Confusing pairs**

(1) adopt—accept
adapt—fit
(2) affect—influence
effect—result
(3) cast—throw
caste—a social group
(4) cheque—order of cash
check—prevent
(5) cost—value
coast—shore
(6) course—route
coarse—rough
(7) decease—die
disease—illness
(8) descent—climbing down
decent—good

3. **Ask your parent**
leaf, flower, fruit, pollen, calyx, stamen, pollination, cell, germinate, thorn, protoplasm, stem, branches.

EXCERCISES

I. Find suitable words from the last page for the following expressions.
(a) unimportant (b) unperishable

An: (a) _______

(b) _______

II. Find five words and their meanings which come between 'infamous' and 'ingratitude'. You may use a dictionary.

An: (a)

(b)

(c)

(d)

III. State the difference between the words given in each pair.

(a) disease
decease

(b) adapt
adept

An: (a)

(b)

Course – 10

1. **Confusing pairs**

   1. foreword—preface
      forward—onward
   2. grand—fine, great
      grant—gift
   3. idle—lazy
      idol—image
   4. lessen—decrease
      lesson—chapter
   5. lose—miss
      loose—free
   6. meat—flesh
      meet—see
   7. momentary—short lived
      momentous—important
   8. pray—beg
      prey—victim

2. **Ask your parent**

I. asafoetida, turmeric, vinegar, benzoin, bitumen, cardamom, pepper, salt, basil, yeast, saffron, ginger.

II. turtle, adder, crab, earthworm, cobra, bug, chameleon, snail, lizard, beetle, ant, frog, louse, leech, butterfly, scorpion, fish, dove, white-ant, bee, mosquito, fly, spider, snake, viper, firefly.

III. armlet, bangle, hair-pin, ring, bracelet, wristlet, anklet, necklace, chain, ear-stud, neck band

EXCERCISES

I. Give the difference in meaning of the words given in each pair. You may use a dictionary.

(a) fore
for

(b) lose
loose

An: (a)

(b)

II. Use in sentence.

(a) anklet (b) scorpion

(c) cardamom (d) cobra

An: (a)

(b)

(c)

(d)

Course-11

1. **Meaning**

jealous	–	envious	journal	–	periodical
job	–	profession	jungle	–	forest

2. **Confusing pairs**

(1) principal—chief
principle—ideal

(2) price—cost
prize—reward

(3) repel—drive back
repeal—cancel

(4) root—basis
route—path

(5) soar—go up
sore—painful

(6) story—tale
storey—floor

(7) team—group
teem—be full

(8) vacation—holidays
vocation—profession

(9) weak—not strong
week—seven days

3. **Ask your parents**

I. dew, fog, frost, gale, hail, haze, rain, lightning, rainbow, smoke, snow, sunshine, thunder.

II. pen, paper, card, paper weight, ink, file, gum, clip, postage stamp, carbon paper, map, nib, compasses, tape, magazine, newspaper, eraser, punch, glue, ink-pad, rubber stamp, holder.

EXCERCISES

I. Write any five words and their meanings which come between 'journal' and 'jungle'. You may use a dictionary.

An: (a)
(b)
(c)
(d)
(e)

II. clearly show the difference between:

(a) repel
repeal

(b) root
route

An: (a)

(b)

III. Use in sentence:

(a) dew (b) glue

(c) smoke (d) map

An: (a)

(b)

(c)

(d)

1. **Meaning**

keen—sharp

knit—weave

2. **Word formation**

(1) *prefixes*

(a) a—on

E.g: a + fresh=afresh

a + mid=amid

(b) ante—before

E.g: ante + diluvian=ante diluvian

ante + meridiem=ante meridiem

(c) anti—against

E.g: anti + communist=anti communist

anti + natural=antinatural

(d) auto—self

E.g: auto + mobile=automobile

auto + biography=autobiography

3. **Ask your parent**

head, body, tail, finger, toe, eye, heart, heel, lip, thump, shoulder, temple, ear, throat, neck, knee, cheek, skin, chest, liver, tongue, jaw, chin, beard, tooth, nail, brain, nose, nostril.

EXCERCISES

I. Write any three words and their meanings which come between 'keen' and 'knit' in your dictionary.

An: (a)

(b)

(c)

II. Write any two words as examples each for the following prefixes. You may use a dictionary. But don't use the very same words appeared in the last page.

(a) ante (b) anti

(c) a (d) auto

An: (a) ________ ________

(b) ________ ________

(c) ________ ________

(d) ________ ________

III. Use in sentence.

(a) knee (b) chin

An: (a)

(b)

Course-13

1. **Meaning**

lack—shortage
large—big
lass—girl
last—final
lazy—idle
lean—thin
learn—study
lesson—chapter
luck—fortune
lure—temptation

2. **Word formation**

(1) *Prefixes*

(a) bi—two

E.g: bi + monthly=bimonthly
bi + lateral=bilateral

(b) co—with

E.g: co + worker=coworker
co + operation=cooperation

(c) de—down

E.g: de + promote=depromote
de + fame=defame

3. **Ask your parent**

Belly, foot, hair, stomach, eye brow, heart, whiskers, palm, gum, fist, blood, mouth, bone, forehead.

EXCERCISES

I. Write two meanings each for the following words other than given above.

(a) learn (b) luck
(c) large

An: (a) ________ ________

(b) ________ ________

(c) ________ ________

II. Write two examples each for the following prefixes. You may use a dictionary. But don't use the very same examples given above.

(a) co- (b) de-

(c) bi-

An: (a) ________ ________

(b) ________ ________

(c) ________ ________

III. Use in sentence.

(a) palm (b) blood

An: (a)

(b)

Course-14

1. **Word formation**

(1) *Prefixes*

(a) ex—out of

E.g: ex + official=ex-official

ex + minister=ex-minister

(b) il—not

E.g: il + luck=illuck

il + legal=illegal

(c) im—not

E.g: im + proper=improper

im + personal=impersonal

(d) in—not

E.g: in + decent=indecent

in + numerable=innumerable

(e) inter—between

E.g: inter + caste=intercaste

inter + department=interdepartment

2. **Ask your parent**

courtyard, portico, sitting room, verandah, door, fireplace, attic, room, window, granary, ante-chamber, chimney, urinal, floor, kitchen, bath-room, stair, bed-room, reading-room

EXCERCISES

I. Use in sentence.

(a) granary (b) floor

(c) bathroom.

An: (a) (b)

(c)

II. Write two examples each for the following prefixes. You may use a dictionary. But don't use the very same examples given above.

(a) inter- (b) il-

(c) in- (d) ex

An: (a) __________ __________

(b) __________ __________

(c) __________ __________

(d) __________ __________

Course-15

1. **Meaning**

mad	– insane	meek	– mild
magnificient	– spelndid	mend	– repair
manage	– handle	merry	– cheerful
manifest	– reveal	mimic	– initiate
margin	– edge	mingle	– mix
master	– leader	mock	– ridicule
meal	– food	money	– wealth

2. **Word formation**

(1) prefixes

(a) mis—ill

E.g: mis + place=misplace
mis + understand=misunderstand

(b) mono—alone

E.g: mono + block=monoblock
mono + gamy=monogamy

(c) non—not

E.g: non + vegetarian=non-vegetarian
non + violent=non-violent

(d) over—very much

E.g: over + power=overpower
over + fear=overfear

3. **Ask your parent**

cholera, consumption, swelling, small-pox, lame, plague, cataract, typhoid, paralysis, headache, asthma, pimple, fever, obesity, giddiness, bald, dumb, tumour.

EXCERCISES

I. Use in sentence.

(a) swelling (b) plague
(c) asthma

An: (a) (b)
(c)

II. What is typhoid?

An:

III. Find correct word from the last page for the following expressions.

(a) joyous (b) manifest

An: (a) ________ (b) ________

IV. Write three words having the prefix 'inter'.

An: ________ ________

____

V. Connect the followings.

(a) non + combatant (b) over + cast

(c) over + look (d) mono + gram

(e) mis + fire

An: (a) ________ (b) ________

(c) ________ (d) ________

(e) ________

Course-16

1. Meaning

neat	–	tidy
necessary	–	essential
need	–	require
notion	–	idea
nought	–	nothing
nude	–	naked

2. Word formation

(1) prefixes

(a) pre—before

E.g: pre + degree = pre-degree

pre + fix = prefix

(b) re—again

E.g: re + examination = reexamination

re + valuation = revaluation

(c) semi—half

E.g: semi + government = semigovernment

semi + classical =semiclassical

(d) sub—under

E.g: sub + division = sub-division

sub + office = sub-office

3. Ask your parent

I. fever, diabetes, piles, elephantiasis, thirst, mad, insomnia, anaemia, cough, worms, leprosy, jaundice, goitre, blind.

II. drum, bugle, bell, cymbal, piano, flute, whistle, harmonium, guitar, violin.

EXCERCISES

I. Connect.

(a) re + condition (b) re + gain

An: (a) (b)

II. Use in sentence.

(a) cough (b) blindness

(c) bell (d) guitar

An: (a)

(b)

(c)

(d)

III. Who is an anaemic?

An:

IV. Write any to words and their meanings which come between 'need' and 'notion' in your dictionary.

An: (a)

(b)

V. What is the meaning of 'vice'?

An:

Course-17

1. **Meaning**

object—protest
observe—notice
obstacle—hindrance
obtain—get
obvious—clear
occur—happen
odd—strange
odour—smell
opaque—not clear
origin—derivation
outcome—result
outlook—view
overthrow—defeat
ox—bullock

2. **Word formation**

(1) prefixes

(a) un—not

E.g: un + common = uncommon
un + belief = unbelief

(b) vice—in the place of

E.g: vice + principal = vice-principal
vice + chancellor = vice-chancellor

(2) suffixes

(a) -age

E.g: mileage, acreage

(b) -ance/-ence

E.g: innoncence, significance

(c) -dom

E.g: kingdon, wisdom

3. **Ask your parent**

Father, mother, brother, sister, son, daughter, uncle, aunt, grand-father, grand-mother, son-in-law, sister-in-law.

EXCERCISES

I. Write three synonyms of the following words. You may use a dictionary.

(a) odd (b) obvious
(c) object

An: (a) (b)
(c)

II. Write two words each for the following prefixes.
(a) vice (b) un

An: (a) ________ ________
(b) ________ ________

III. Use in sentence.
(a) aunt (b) son

An: (a)

(b)

IV. Whom is a sister-in-law called to?

An:

V. Leela's daughter is Radha. Who is Leela to Radha?

Course-18

1. **Meaning**

pact—treaty
pamphlet—booklet
pants—trousers
pardon—forgiveness
pass—go
passion—emotion
path—way
pathetic—tragic
pattern—model
peasant—farmer
peep—look secretly
per—each
perceive—understand
perfect—faultless
perish—die
persuade—induce
petition—request
petty—silly
pirate—sea rober
place—-seat
plea—request
pleasure—happiness
plural—more than one
portion—part
possess—owe
pot—vessel
prestige—dignity

2. **Word formation**

(1) Suffixes

(a) -hood
E.g: brotherhood, childhood
(b) -ion
E.g: creation, recreation
(c) -ism
E.g: communism, socialism
(d) -ment
E.g: movement, excitement

3. **Ask your parent**

Rose, lily, jasmine, lilac, lotus, dehlia, daisy, sunflower, poppy, pandanus.

EXCERCISES

I. Use in sentence.
(a) poppy (b) jasmine

An: (a)

(b)

II. Write all the meanings of the following words. You may use a dictionary.

(a) perfect (b) profound

(c) protest

An: (a)

(b)

(c)

III. Which flower do you like most?

An:

IV. Name the flowers grow in your courtyard.

An:

Course-19

1. **Meaning**

pride—arrogance
prime—principal
prison—jail
private—secret
prize—reward
proficient—expert
profound—deep
prohibit—prevent
proper—right
proprietor—owner
protest—object
provide—give
provisional—temporary

2. **Word formation**

(1) Noun forming suffixes
(a) -ness
E.g: brightness, keenness
(b) -ship
E.g: fellowship, friendship
(c) -tude
E.g: altitude, attitude

3. **Ask your parent**

guest, owner, tenant, teacher, customer, disciple, host, heir, merchant, pleader, landlord, farmer, soldier, engineer, magician, sailor, postman, author, banker, book-seller, artist, washerman, nurse, druggist, tailor, doctor, inspector, baker, watchman, grocer, clerk, printer, boatman, beggar, barrister, manager, publisher, cook, painter, physician, barber, editor.

EXCERCISES

I. Write three words each having the following suffixes.
(a) -tude (b) -ness
(c) -ship

An: (a) ________ ________ ________
(b) ________ ________ ________
(c) ________ ________ ________

II. Use in sentence.
(a) pleader (b) merchant
(c) editor

An: (a)

(b)

(c)

III. Gopi went to a stationary shop and bought an umbrella. Who is Gopi to the shopkeeper?

An:

IV. Define a landlord. You may use a dictionary.

An:

Course-20

1. **Meaning**

quantity	– size or amount	recent	– new
quarrel	– dispute	reckon	– guess
quest	– search	recommend	– advise
quick	– fast	rectify	– lower
quit	– leave	refrain	– obstain
race	– speed contest	refuse	– reject
raid	– attack	regard	– consider
raise	– liftup	regular	– normal
rapport	– harmony	release	– set free
rare	– uncommon	relinguish	– give up
ratify	– confirm	rely	– trust
reach	– arrive at	remote	– distant
rear	– back part	render	– submit
rebate	– discount	renown	– fame
recall	– remember	repeal	– cancel

2. **Word formation**

(1) Noun forming suffixes

(a) -y

E.g: spongy, curdy

(b) -er/-or

E.g: controller, orator

3. **Ask your parent**

shirt, pants, hat, belt, sleeve, blanket, lace, shawl, hand-kerchief, gloves, knickers, towel, sheet, muffler, button, turban, waist coat.

EXCERCISES

I. Write any three words and their meanings which come between 'regular' and 'release'.

An: (a)

(b)

(c)

II. Use in sentence.

(a) blanket (b) gloves

An: (a)

(b)

III. What is a lace?

An:

IV. Write all the meanings of the following words which can be seen in your dictionary.

(a) quest (b) rebate

An: (a)

(b)

Course-21

1. **Meaning**

repine	–	complain	scheme	–	plan
reply	–	answer	section	–	division
repulse	–	repel	seize	–	grasp
rescue	–	save	seldom	–	rarely
resign	–	give up	select	–	choose
resist	–	oppose	shout	–	cry aloud
resume	–	continue	siesta	–	mid-day sleep
retreat	–	move back	signify	–	mean
return	–	come back	snare	–	trap
reveal	–	make clear	sole	–	entirely
reverie	–	day dream	soul	–	spirit
rude	–	vulgar	source	–	origin
rule	–	govern	speculate	–	guess
sage	–	wise	spoil	–	damage
same	–	identical	sport	–	game
sample	–	specimen	spouse	–	husband or wife
savage	–	wild	stance	–	manner
save	–	rescue			

2. **Ask your parent**

I: mango, pineapple, pomegrenate, apple, grape, orange, lemon, plum, jack fruit, watermelon, apricot.

II: gauge, lancet, rudder, divider, screw-driver, spade, shovel, fishing-angle, axe, saw, razor, scissors, chisel, hammer, mallet.

EXECERCISES

I. Define a siesta. You may use a dictionary.

An:

II. What is a grape?

An:

III. Take a dictionary and extract the entries given at the following words.

(a) apple (b) lemon
(c) spade (d) axe

An: (a)

(b)

(c)

(d)

IV. Use in sentence.

(a) spoil (b) resume

An: (a)

(b)

Course-22

1. **Meaning**

state	–	condition	tell	–	say
statue	–	law	tempest	–	storm
stern	–	severe	tempt	–	persuade
stop	–	prevent	test	–	examine
strange	–	odd	theme	–	principal idea
stress	–	emphasis			
subdue	–	overcome	thick	–	dense
subject	–	topic	thing	–	matter
sum	–	total	through	–	perfect
sundry	–	various	throw	–	fling
supervise	–	oversee	tidy	–	neat
support	–	assist	timid	–	shy
sure	–	certain	title	–	heading
surmise	–	guess	toffee	–	sweet
survive	–	outlive	token	–	symbol
suspect	–	doubt	toll	–	tax
swift	–	rapid	tomb	–	grave
synopsis	–	summary	total	–	whole
system	–	method	tough	–	hard
task	–	work	trade	–	business
team	–	group	true	–	real

2. **Ask Your parent**

Potato, cucumber, pumpkin, mushroom, carrot, onion, couliflower, cabbage, chilli, raddish, bean, tomatio, ladies finger.

I. Write the names of vegetables which are in use at your kitchen.

Ans:

II. Use in sentence.

(a) sum (b) token (c) thick (d)

Ans: (a)

(b)

(c)

(d)

III. Define a 'synopsis'. You may use a dictionary.

Ans:

IV. What is the past form of 'suspect'? You may use a dictionary.

Ans:

Course - 23

1. **Meaning**

trust — believe
truth — reality
twice — double
ugly — deformed
ultimate — final
unable — not capable
uncommon — rare
under — beneath
undesirable — unpleasant
unhappy — not happy

2. **Word formation**

(1) Noun forming suffixes

(a) -ate/-ite

E.g: migrate, invite

(b) -en

E.g: lengthen, flatten

(c) -ise/-ize

E.g: capitalize, neutralize

3. **Ask your parent**

I: husband, wife, nephew, niece, step-mother, step-father, mother-in-law, father-in-law, daughter-in-law, adopted son, adopted daughter.

II: needle, soap, phial, bowl, dish, candle, sack, bench, bucket, pot, box, mirror, plate, oven, tooth brush, safe, lock, key, comb, chair, jar, tumbler, spoon, tongs, stove, mortar, almirah.

EXCERCISES

I. Rajan married Radha, who is Rajan to Radha and Radha to Rajan?

An:

II. Suresh had no children. So he adopted a child named Sudha. Say, who is Suresh to Sudha?

An:

III. Use in sentence.

(a) soap (b) spoon

An: (a)

(b)

IV. Give two words each having the following suffixes.

(a) -en (b) -ate

An: (a) ________ ________

(b) ________ ________

Course-24

1. **Meaning**

unique—unequal
unusual—uncommon
uphold—support
uttered—shouted
vacuum—empty
vague—unclear
vain—worthless
valiant—courageous
value—cost
vanish—disappear
vast—very large

2. **Word formation**

(1) Adjective forming suffixes

(a) -al

E.g: neutral, legal

(b) -able/-ible/-ble

E.g: movable, audible

(c) -ful

E.g: tearful, sorrowful

(d) -ish

E.g: childish, foolish

(e) -less

E.g: heartless, hopeless

(f) -ous

E.g: dangerous, vigorous

3. **Ask your parent**

broth, break-fast, tea, cake, ice-cream, meal, curry, pickle, coffee, curd, lunch, cheese, biscuit, feast, food, butter, meat, mutton, pork, chicken, supper, bread, dinner, beef.

EXCERCISES

I. Write the noun forming suffixes that you have studied. Give two examples for each other than given in this book.

An:

II. What is a curd?

An:

III. Use in sentence.

(a) pickle (b) value

(c) beef

An: (a)

(b)

(c)

Course-25

1. **Meaning**

venom	—	snake poison
venture	—	adventurous effort
verdict	—	court order
verse	—	poem

2. **Word formation**

(1) adverb forming suffixes

(a) -ly

E.g: cordially, amicably

(b) -ce

E.g: once, twice

(c) -st

E.g: midst, betwixt

(d) -ward

E.g: southward, backward

(2) Compound words

(a)noun + noun

E.g: table lamp, bed sheet

(b) adjective + noun

E.g: chief guest, main stream

EXCERCISES

I. Give two words each having the following suffixes.

(a) -st (b) -ward

(c) -ce

An: (a) ________ ________

(b) ________ ________

(c) ________ ________

II. Use in sentence.

(a) voice (b) venom

An: (a)

(b)

III. What is a verdict?

An:

IV. Form two compound words using the following formulae.
noun + noun.

An: ________

____

Course-26

1. Meaning

wage	—	payment
want	—	require
warm	—	hot
weary	—	tired
weep	—	cry
withdraw	—	take back
worth	—	deserving
wrong	—	incorrect
yield	—	surrender
zeal	—	enthusiasm

2. Word formation

(1) Compound words

(a) preposition + noun

E.g: in-land, down-hill

(b) present participle + noun

E.g: working woman, doing business

3.Ask your parent

rice, wheat, gram, sugar, oat, barley, oil, pulse, millet, maize, lentil, molasses, mustard.

EXCERCISES

I. Use in sentence.

(a) wrong (b) want

(c) worth

An: (a)

(b)

(c)

II. What is lentil?

An:

III. What is the difference between 'rice' and 'gram'?

An:

IV. What are the adverb forming suffixes? Give two examples for each.

An:

HOME STUDY SERIES - 2

PRONUNCIATION AND PARTS OF SPEECH

P. V. GOPALAKRISHNAN

PRONUNCIATION

CONTENTS

Sl. No.	Chapters	Exercise written date					Marks	Remarks
1.	Phonetic Symbols							
2.	Correct Pronounciation of some words							
3.	Rules Related to Pronunciation							
4.	Stress							
5.	Double Pronunciation							
6.	Practice							

1
Phonetic Symbols

ɪ: **as in** bee /bi:/
ɪ **as in** bit /bɪt/
e **as in** den /den/
æ **as in** mat /m æ t/
ɑ: **as in** farm /fɑ:m/
ɒ **as in** got /gɒt/
ʊ **as in** put /pʊt/
u: **as in** moon /mu:n/
ʌ **as in** love /lʌv/
ɜ: **as in** burn /bɜ:n/
ə **as in** another /ə'nʌðə*/
eɪ **as in** age /eidʒ/
əʊ **as in** no /nəʊ/
ɑɪ **as in** dive /daɪv/
ɑʊ **as in** how /haʊ/
ɔɪ **as in** boil /bɔɪl/

EXERCISES

I. Write five words which start from the sound /æ/. You may use an English Pronouncing Dictionary (EPD).

Ans: __________ __________ __________
__________ __________

II. Find the phonetic symbol for the vowels in the following words.

(1) hit	(2) man	(3) moon
(4) car	(5) dare	(6) love

Ans:

(1)	(2)	(3)
(4)	(5)	(6)

III. Give one example each for the phonetic symbols given above. Don't use the very same words given above.

Ans: ɪ: __________ ɪ __________
e __________ æ __________
ɑ: __________ ɒ __________

ʊ ___________	u: ___________
ʌ ___________	ɜ: ___________
ə ___________	ei ___________
əʊ ___________	ai ___________
aʊ ___________	ɔɪ ___________

Phonetic Symbols (cont.)

ɪə **as in** hear /hɪə*/
eə **as in** pair /peə*/
ʊə **as in** cure /kjʊə*/
p **as in** pen /pen/
b **as in** bed /bed/
t **as in** to /tu:/
d **as in** do /du:/
k **as in** come /kʌm/
g **as in** get /get/
tʃ **as in** chill /tʃɪl/
dʒ **as in** jelly /dʒeli/
f **as in** five /faɪv/
v **as in** love /lʌv/
θ **as in** think /θɪŋk/
ð **as in** this /ðɪs/

EXERCISES

I. Write three examples for each of the following sounds.
/t//tʃ//θ/

Ans: ___________ ___________ ___________
___________ ___________ ___________
___________ ___________ ___________

II. Write down the phonetic symbol for the first consonant letter in each of the following words.

(a) gas	(b) voice	(c) tip
(d) those	(e) drive	(f) poison

Ans: (a) ___________ (b) ___________
(c) ___________ (d) ___________
(e) ___________ (f) ___________

III. Write one example each for words containing the following phonetic symbols.

(a) /f/	(b) /k/	(c) /eə/
(d) /dʒ/	(e) /b/	

Ans: (a) __________ (b) __________
(c) __________ (d) __________
(e) __________

Phonetic Symbols (cont.)

s **as in** in see /si:/
z **as in** zoo /zu:/
ʃ **as in** ship /ʃɪp/
ʒ **as in** measure /meʒə*/
h **as in** hit /hɪt/
m **as in** man /mæn/
n **as in** nil /nɪl/
ŋ **as in** fling /fliŋ/
l **as in** lip /lɪp/
ɤ **as in** red /ɤed/
j **as in** you /ju:/
w **as in** well /wel/

EXERCISES

I. Write five examples for each sound given below.
/h/ /ℓ/ /n/

Ans: __________ __________ __________
__________ __________ __________
__________ __________ __________
__________ __________ __________
__________ __________ __________

II. Write down the phonetic symbols of the first letter given in each of the following words.
(a) road (b) rail
(c) main (d) mind
(e) zeal (f) water
(g) wander.

Ans: (a) __________ (b) __________
(c) __________ (d) __________
(e) __________ (f) __________
(g) __________

III. Write three examples of English words for the /z/ sound.

Ans: __________ __________
____

2
Correct Pronunciation of Some Words

abbreviate — /ə'brɪ:vɪeɪt/
accommodate — /ə'kɒmə'deɪt/
achieve — /ə'tʃi:v/
acquiesce — /ɪæ'kwɪ'es/
across — /ə'krɒs/
address — /ə'dress/
affectionately — /ə'fekʃnətlɪ/
agreeable — /ə'grɪəbl/
although — /ə:l'ðəʊ/
always — /ɔ:lweɪz/
ancient — /'eɪnʃənt/
angel — /eɪndʒəl/
anxiety — /æŋ'zaɪətɪ/
appear — /ə'pɪə*/
argument — /'ɑ:gjʊmənt/
ascent — /ə'sent/
avaricious — /ævə'rɪʃəs/
balloon — /bə'lu:n/
beautiful — /'bju:təfʊl/

EXERCISES

I. Write phonetic transcription for the following words. You may use an EPD.

(1) absorb (2) absurd
(3) admit (4) advance
(5) amoeba (6) anus
(7) around (8) attain
(9) aurora (10) avoid
(11) await (12) azure

Ans: (1) ________ (2) ________
(3) ________ (4) ________
(5) ________ (6) ________

(7) __________ (8) __________

(9) __________ (10) __________

(11) __________ (12) __________

II. Write English words for the following transcriptions.

(a) /'eniwei/ (b) /'æpɤəʊ/ (c) /ɔ:ı/

Ans: (a) __________ (b) __________ (c) __________

III. Correct the followings.

(a) /ə'kɤɔ:s/ (b) /'pıə*/ (c) /ə'tʃi:v/

Ans: (a) __________ (b) __________ (c) __________

Correct Pronunciation of Some Words (cont).

believe — /bılı:v/
biscuit — /'bıskıt/
boiled — /bɔıld/
break — /bɤeık/
budget — /'bʌdʒıt/
business — /'bıznıs/
carrying — /kæɤııŋ/
caught — /kɔ:t/
ceiling — /sı:lıŋ/
cemetery —/'semıtɤı/
choose — /tʃu:z/
clothes — /kləʊðz/
colour — /'kʌlə/
commemorate — /kə'meməɤeıt/
compliments — /'kɒmplıments/
condemn — /kən'dem/
control — /kən'tɤəʊl/
convenience — /kən'vı:njəns/
council —/kaʊnsıl/
course — /kɔ:s/

EXERCISES

I. Write English words for the following transcriptions.

(a) /'bɤeıslıt/ (b) /bʊk/

(c) /'bı:tl/ (d) /bɔ:l/

(e) /bɔ:n/

Ans: (a) __________ (b) __________

(c) __________ (d) __________

(e) __________

II. Write phonetic transcriptions for the following words.

(a) boss (b) breed
(c) bus (d) calcium
(e) child (f) chess
(g) goat (h) compact

Ans: (a) __________ (b) __________
(c) __________ (d) __________
(e) __________ (f) __________
(g) __________ (h) __________

III. Correct the followings.

(a) /bɔ:ild/ (b) /'biskət/
(c) /tʃu:s/

Ans: (a) __________ (b) __________
(c) __________

Correct Pronunciation of Some Words (cont.)

cutting — /'kʌtɪŋ/
deceive — /dɪ'si:v/
democracy — /dɪ'mɒkɤəsɪ/
describe — /dɪ'skɤaɪb/
dessert — /dɪ'zɜ:t/
development — /dɪ'veləpmənt/
dexterous — /'dekstəɤəs/
discreet — /dɪ'skɤrɪ't/
disease — dɪ'zɪ:s/
drily — /'dɤaɪlɪ/
ecstasy — /'ekstəsɪ/
elephant — /'elɪfənt/
embarrass — /ɪm'bæɤəs/
emphasize — /'emfəsaɪz/
engineer — /eɳdʒɪ'ɳɪə*/
exaggerate — /ɪg'zædʒəɤeɪt/
excellent — /'eksələnt/
exhaust — /ɪg'zɔ:st/
existance — /ɪg'zɪstəns/
explanation — /eksplə'neɪʃn/
extreme — /ɪk'stɤɪ:m/

EXERCISES

I. Correct the followings.

(a) /ek'stɤrɪ:m/ (b) /'elɪfənt/
(c) /kɒtɪŋ/ (d) /endʒɪ'nɪ:ə*/
(e) /dɪ'si:s/

Ans: (a) __________ (b) __________
(c) __________ (d) __________
(e) __________

II. Write phonetic transcriptions for the following words.

(a) discuss (b) doze
(c) dual (d) echo
(e) edit (f) empty
(g) endure (h) equal
(i) except

Ans: (a) __________ (b) __________
(c) __________ (d) __________
(e) __________ (f) __________
(g) __________ (h) __________
(i) __________

III. Write English words for the following phonetic transcriptions.

(a) /dɪ'sɜ:n/ (b) /dɪ'vaɪd/
(c) /dʌf/ (d) /'edɪbl/

Ans: (a) __________ (b) __________
(c) __________ (d) __________

Correct Pronunciation of some words (cont.)

favourite — /'feɪvəɤɪt/
foreign — /'fɒɤən/
freight — /fɤaɪt/
fulfil — /fʊlfɪl/
gauge — /geɪdʒ/
gaiety — /geɪətɪ/
gallop — /gæləp/
gaol — /dʒeɪl/
government — /'gʌvr:mənt/
grief — /gɤɪ:f/
harass — /hæɤəs/
heal — /hɪ:l/
heard — /hɜ:d/
height — /haɪt/
hideous — /'hɪdɪəs/
humour — /'hju:mə*/

hypocrisy — /hɪ'pɒkɤəsɪ/
imposter — /ɪm'pɒstə*/
incite — /ɪnsaɪt/
initial — /ɪ'nɪʃl/
inquire — /ɪn'kwaɪə*/
interrupt — /ɪntə'ɤʌpt/
inventor — /ɪnvəntɤ*/

EXERCISE

I. Write phonetic transcriptions for the following words.

(a) govern (b) grief
(c) guest (d) half
(e) harm (f) herd
(g) hook (h) hurt
(i) include

Ans: (a) __________ (b) __________
(c) __________ (d) __________
(e) __________ (f) __________
(g) __________ (h) __________
(i) __________

II. Correct the followings.

(a) /ɪnɪʃəl/ (b) /ɪnvɒntɤ/
(c) /dʒɑɪl/ (d) /fɤeɪt/
(e) /heɪt/

Ans: (a) __________ (b) __________
(c) __________ (d) __________
(e) __________

III. Write English words for the following phonetic transcriptions.

(a) /fɔ:lt/ (b) /fɪfə/
(c) /'gɑ:mə/

Ans: (a) __________ (b) __________
(c) __________

Correct Pronunciation of Some Words (cont.)

jealous — /'dʒeləs/
jewellery — /'dʒu:əlɤɪ/
journey — /'dʒɜ:nɪ/
judge — /dʒʌdʒ/
kaleidoscope — /kə'lɑɪləskəʊp/
kidnap — /'kɪdnæp/
kindergarten — /'kɪndə,gɑ:tn/
knave — /neɪv/

knelt — /nelt/
knife — /naɪf/
knot — /nɒt/
knowledge — /ˈnɒlɪdʒ/
labour — /ˈleɪbə*/
laundry — /ˈlɔ:ndrɪ/
league — /li:g/
leisure — /ˈleʒə*/
lettuce — /ˈletɪs/
license — /ˈlaɪsəns/
lieutenant — /lefˈtenəʌt/
lightning — /ˈlaɪtnɪŋ/
likelihood — /ˈlaɪklɪhʊd/
loose — /lʊ:s/
lying — /ˈlaɪɪŋ/

EXERCISE

I. Write phonetic transcriptions for the following words.

(a) join (b) journey
(c) joy (d) judge
(e) key (f) kill
(g) kith (h) know
(i) lack (j) lake

Ans: (a) ________ (b) ________
(c) ________ (d) ________
(e) ________ (f) ________
(g) ________ (h) ________
(i) ________ (j) ________

II. Correct the followings.

(a) /nɒlt/ (b) /ˈletu:s/
(c) /lus/ (d) /ˈlaɪsɒns/

Ans: (a) ________ (b) ________
(c) ________ (d) ________

III. Write English words for the following phonetic transcriptions.

(a) /lɑ:f/ (b) /leɪ/
(c) /kɪnʃɪp/

Ans: (a) ________ (b) ________
(c) ________

Correct Pronunciation of some words (cont.)

manoeuvre — /mə'nu:və*/
massacre — /'mæsəkə*/
meant — /ment/
mercenary — /'mɜ:sɪnəɤɪ/
mileage — /'mɑɪlɪdʒ/
mischief — /'mɪstʃɪf/
missionary — /'mɪʃnəɤɪ/
misspell — /mɪs'spel/
monotonous — /mə'nɒtnəs/
movable — /'mu:vəbl/
necessary — /'nesəsəɤɪ/
niece — /nɪ:s/
novice — /'nɒvɪs/
nuisance — /'nju:sns/
obedient — /ə'bɪ:djənt/
obvious — /'ɒbvɪəs/
occurred — /ə'kɜ:d/
opposite — /'ɒpəzɪt/
original — /ə'rɪdʒənʌl/
paralyse — /p'æɤəlɑɪz/
parliament — /'pa:ləmənt/
pastime — /'pa:staɪm/
pedlar — /'pedlə*/
persuasion — /pə'sweɪʒn/

EXERCISES

I. Write phonetic symbols for the underlined letter(s) in the following words.

(a) niece (b) obvious
(c) opposite

Ans: (a) ________ (b) ________
(c) ________

II. Write phonetic transcriptions for the following words.

(a) month (b) new
(c) number (d) odd.

Ans: (a) ________ (b) ________
(c) ________ (d) ________

III. Correct the followings.

(a) /'məɪlədʒ/ (b) /nɪ:z/

(c) /ɔ'kɜ:d/ (d) /pədlə*/

Ans: (a) __________ (b) __________

(c) __________ (d) __________

IV. Write English words for the following phonetic transcriptions.

(a) /mæml/ (b) /mə'ɤu:n/

(c) /neɪtɪv/ (d) /ɒf/

Ans: (a) __________ (b) __________

(c) __________ (d) __________

Correct Pronunciation of Some Words (cont.)

perspire — /pə'spɑɪə*/

phantom — /'fæntəm/

piece — /pi:s/

pigeon — /'pɪdʒɪn/

pleasure — /'pleʒə*/

possession — /pə'zeʃn/

potato — /pə'teɪtəʊ/

pray — /pɤeɪ/

precede — /ˌpɤɪ:'sɪ:d/

privilege — /'prɪvɪlɪdʒ/

proceed — /pɤə'sɪ:d/

profession — /pɤə'feʃn/

progeny — /'pɤɒdʒənɪ/

pursuit — /pə'sju:t/

quarrel — /'kwɒɤəl/

queue — /kju:/

quick — /kwɪk/

receipt — /rɪ'si:t/

receive — /rɪ'si:v/

refer — /rɪ'fɜ:*/

relief — /rɪ'li:v/

religion — /rɪ'lɪdʒən/

EXERCISES

I. Write English words for the following phonetic transcriptions.

(a) /peɪpə*/ (b) /pænkɤɪ'əs/

(c) /pi:ən/ (d) /kwɪlt/

(e) /ri:bɪ'ɪd/ (f) /rɪ'pɤu:f/

Ans: (a) __________ (b) __________
(c) __________ (d) __________
(e) __________ (f) __________

II. Write phonetic symbols for the letter(s) underlined in the following words.

(a) rigid (b) pursuit
(c) pharmaceutic

Ans: (a) __________ (b) __________
(c) __________

III. Write phonetic transcription for the following words.

(a) passage (b) pill
(c) plume (d) quiet
(e) record

Ans: (a) __________ (b) __________
(c) __________ (d) __________
(e) __________

IV. Correct the followings.

(a) /pɤaɪ/ (b) /ɤəli:v/

Ans: (a) __________ (b) __________

Correct Pronunciation of Some Words (cont.)

representative — /ˌɤepɤɪ'zentətɪv/
rhyme — /ɤaɪm/
road — /ɤəʊd/
rogue — /ɤəʊg/
sale — /seɪl/
scene — /si:n/
secrecy — /'si:kɤəsɪ/
seize — /si:z/
sergeant — /'sa:dʒənt/
shoes — /su:z/
shyly — /ʃaɪlɪ/
simultaneous — /ˌsɪməl'teɪnjəs/
skill — /skɪl/
slyly — /'slaɪlɪ/
solemn — /'sɒləm/
sovereign — /'sɒvɤɪn/
steal — /stɪ:l/
storey — /'stɔ:ɤɪ/

straight — /'stɤeɪt/
strength — /'stɤeŋθ/
subtilty — /'sʌtltɪ/

EXERCISES

I. Correct the followings.

(a) /sɪ:s/ (b) /ʃu:s/
(c) /ɤəɪm/ (d) /'sɔləm/

Ans: (a) __________ (b) __________
(c) __________ (d) __________

II. Write English words for the following phonetic transcriptions.

(a) /ɤʌst/ (b) /ɤʊɪn/
(c) /self/ (d) /si:/
(e) /'səvɤəl/

Ans: (a) __________ (b) __________
(c) __________ (d) __________
(e) __________

III. Write phonetic transcriptions for the following words.

(a) room (b) salary
(c) scratch (d) shirt

Ans: (a) __________ (b) __________
(c) __________ (d) __________

IV. Write phonetic symbols for the underlined letter(s) in the following words.

(a) request (b) since
(c) soldier

Ans: (a) __________ (b) __________
(c) __________

Correct Pronunciation of Some Words (cont.)

suicide — /'sʊɪsɑɪd/
sulphur — /'sʌlfə*/
summary — /'sʌməɤɪ/
syllable — /'sɪləbl/
symmetry — /'sɪmətɤɪ/
tail — /teɪl/
tense — /tens/
their — /ðeə*/
threw — /θɤu:/
throne — /θɤəʊn/

through — /θɤu:/
toe — /təʊ/
transferred — /tɤæns'fɜ:d/
traveller — /tɤævlə*/
treacherous — /'tɤetʃəɤəs/
two — /tu:/
vacuum — /'vækjʊəm/
valley — /'vælı/
valour — /'vælə*/
vigorous — /'vıgəɤəs/
villain — /'vılən/
voice — /vɔıs/
volley — /'vɒlı/
vomit — /'vɒmıt/

EXERCISES

I. Write phonetic symbols for the underlined letter(s) in the following words.

(a) subside (b)supreme
(c) tally (d) tense

Ans: (a) __________ (b) __________
(c) __________ (d) __________

II. Write phonetic transcriptions for the following words.

(a) shift (b) tact
(c) table (d) telegraph
(e) turn

Ans: (a) __________ (b) __________
(c) __________ (d) __________
(e) __________

III. Write English words for the following phonetic transcriptions.

(a) /tə'bu:/ (b) /'sıɤıə/
(c) /teıp/ (d) /'tə'rıfık/

Ans: (a) __________ (b) __________
(c) __________ (d) __________

IV. Correct the followings.

(a) /tu/ (b) /taıl/
(c) /vɔ:lı/

Ans: (a) __________ (b) __________
(c) __________

Correct Pronunciation of Some Words (cont).

wagon — /'wægən/
waylaid — /weɪ'leɪd/
wednesday — /'wenzdɪ/
weight — /weɪt/
welfare — /'welfə*/
whole — /həul/
wilful — /'wɪlful/
withdraw — /wɪð'drɔ:/
woe — /wəu/
woollen — /'wulən/
write — /raɪt/
yacht — /jɒt/
yield — /jɪ:ld/
zeal — /zi:l/
zenana — /ze'na:nə/
zero — /'zɪəɤəu/
zoo — /zu:/

EXERCISES

I. Write phonetic transcription for the following words.

(a) watch (b) water
(c) weak (d) while
(e) wit (f) yolk
(g) zoom

Ans: (a) ________ (b) ________
(c) ________ (d) ________
(e) ________ (f) ________
(g) ________

II. Correct the followings.

(a) /si:l/ (b) /su:/
(c) /waɪt/ (d) /wagɔn/

Ans: (a) ________ (b) ________
(c) ________ (d) ________

III. Write English words for the following phonetic transcriptions.

(a) wɪ:l (b) west
(c) zest (d) ju:

Ans: (a) ________ (b) ________
(c) ________ (d) ________

IV. Write phonetic symbols for the underlined letter(s) in the following words.

(a) write (b) yolk

Ans: (a) __________ (b) __________

Correct Pronunciation of Some frequently used Words

a — /eɪ/
all — /ɔ:l/
am — /æm/
an — /æn/
are — /a:*/
as — /æz/
at — /æt/
but — /bʌt/
by — /baɪ/
for — /fɔ:*/
he — /hi:/
her — /hɜ:*/
his — /hɪz/
him — /hɪm/
how — /hɑʊ/
I — /aɪ/
in — /ɪn/
into — /ˈɪntʊ/
it — /ɪt/

EXERCISES

I. Write phonetic transcription for the following words.

(a) by (b) her
(c) his (d) as
(e) an (f) I
(g) it

Ans: (a) __________ (b) __________
(c) __________ (d) __________
(e) __________ (f) __________
(g) __________

II. Write English words for the following phonetic transcriptions.

(a) /æt/ (b) /ˈɪntʊ/
(c) /haʊ/ (d) /bɑɪ/
(e) /ɔ:l/

Ans: (a) __________ (b) __________
(c) __________ (d) __________
(e) __________

III. Correct the followings.
(a) /hɪ/ (b) /bət/
(c) /hɪs/

Ans: (a) __________ (b) __________
(c) __________

Correct Pronunciation of some frequently used words

me — /mi:/
my — /maɪ/
no — /nəʊ/
of — /əv/
on — /ɒn/
or — /ɔ:*/
out — /aʊt/
put — /pʊt/
she — /ʃi:/
so — /səʊ/
to — /tu:/
too — /tu:/
under — /'ʌndə*/
up — /ʌp/
upon — /ə'pɒn/
us — /ʌs/
what — /wɒt/
where — /weə*/
which — /wɪtʃ/
when — /wen/
who — /hu:/
whom — /hu:m/
why — /waɪ/

EXERCISES

I. Write phonetic transcription for the following words.
(a) out (b) she
(c) too (d) which
(e) my (f) whom
(g) us

Ans: (a) ________ (b) ________
(c) ________ (d) ________
(e) ________ (f) ________
(g) ________

II. Write English words for the following phonetic transcriptions.

(a) /ʌp/ (b) /wɒt/
(c) /waɪ/ (d) /pʊt/
(e) /ɔ:*/

Ans: (a) ________ (b) ________
(c) ________ (d) ________
(e) ________

III. Correct the followings.

(a) /ə'uɔ:n/ (b) /wən/
(c) /mɪ/ (d) /meɪ/
(e) /sɔ:/ (f) /we*/

Ans: (a) ________ (b) ________
(c) ________ (d) ________
(e) ________ (f) ________

3

Rules Related to Pronunciation

(1) 'c' which comes before 'e' is normally pronounced together as /s/.

E.g. dance

convince

(2) 'p + h' is normally pronounced as /f/.

E.g. phone

photo

(3) 'b' which comes after 'm' is often unpronounced.

E.g. comb

lamb

(4) Starting 'k' which comes before 'n' is not pronounced.

E.g. know

knee

(5) closed 'o' is uncommon in English.

E.g. board

both

EXERCISES

I. Write the pronunciation in phonetic script of the words given below.

(a) knell (b) knife

(c) knight

Ans: (a)__________ (b) __________

(c) __________

II. Correct the followings

(a) /'pəutəu/ (Photo) (b) /frasal/ (phrasal)

Ans: (a) __________ (b) __________

III. What are the pronunciations of the following letters.

(a) 'b' which comes after 'm'.

(b) p+h

(c) 'k' which comes before 'n'.

(d) o

Ans: (a) __________ (b) __________

(c) __________ (d)__________

IV. Write the pronunciation of 'c' in the following words.

(a) panacea (b) dance

(c) coir.

Ans: (a) __________ (b) __________
(c) __________

Rules related to Pronunciation (cont.)

(1) Final 'e' is often unpronounced.
E.g. dove
love

(2) Starting 'p' is not pronounced if it is preceded by 's' or 't'.
E.g. Psychology
Ptolomy

(3) 'r' is not pronounced fully if it is preceded by a consonant or a pause.
E.g. far
forth

(4) Starting 'h' is not pronounced in some cases.
E.g. honour
hour.

(5) ' i' which comes after t, s, sh are not pronounced normally.
E.g. vision
fashion
nation

EXERCISES

I. Write the pronounciation of the letter(s) underlined in the following words.

(a) o<u>r</u> (b) pen<u>s</u>ion
(c) ca<u>r</u> (d) <u>ph</u>antom
(e) <u>p</u>seudo (f) lon<u>e</u>
(g) <u>h</u>onour

Ans: (a) __________ (b) __________
(c) __________ (d) __________
(e) __________ (f) __________
(g) __________

III. write phonetic transcriptions for the following words.

(a) tension (b) hour
(c) fore (d) psych
(e) revive (f) underline
(g) move (h) keep
(i) one

Ans: (a) __________ (b) __________
(c) __________ (d) __________
(e) __________ (f) __________
(g) __________ (h) __________

Rules related to Pronunciation (cont).

Past tense forming suffix -d/-ed has three types of pronunciation according to the words to whcih they are attached.

(1) /d/—if the past ending is suffixed to a voiced sound.
E.g. Showed Eg — /ʃəʊd/
played — /pleɪd/
(2) /t/– if the past ending is suffixed to a voiceless sound.
E.g. Stopped —/stɒpt/
looked — /lʊkt/
(3) /id/– if the past ending is suffixed to d/t
E.g. ended — /endɪd/
waited —/weɪtɪd/

EXERCISES

I. What are the differences in pronunciation on suffixing past endings to different words. Give examples for each.

Ans:

II. Write phonetic transactions for the following words.
(a) affraighted (b) landed
(c) wanded (d) selected
(e) planned (f) showered
(g) handed

Ans: (a) __________ (b) __________
(c) __________ (d) __________
(e) __________ (f) __________
(g) __________

III. Correct the following pronunciation, if they are incorrect.
(a) Scotched /skɒtʃd/ (b) inverted /ɪn′vɜːtɪd/

Ans: (a) __________ (b) __________

4
Stress

English words are composed of one or more syllable(s). A syllable is a speech unit having one vowel sound and one or more consonant sound(s) at one or either sides.

E.g.

one syllabled word — be
two syllabled word — be/lieve
three syllabled word — be/lieve/ing
four syllabled word — be/lieve/ing/ly
five syllabled word — un/be/lieve/ing/ly

All syllables in a word are not pronounced taking similar force. Where we use more force than needed for the rest, it is called the stressed syllable.

In English there are two types of stresses

(1) Primary Stress.
It is marked as /ˈ/

(2) Secondary stress.
It is marked as /ˌ/

EXERCISES

I. What is a syllable ? Give an example.

Ans:

II. What is stress ? Give one example.

Ans:

III. Divide the following words into syllables.

(a) hand (b) handed
(c) handy (d) unhanded.

Ans: (a) __________ (b) __________
(c) __________ (d) __________

IV. Mark primary stress.

(a) /aɪzək/ (b) /ɳaɪlɒn/

(c) /rɪvet/ (d) /tenə˞t/

Ans: (a) __________ (b) __________

(c) __________ (d) __________

Given below are two examples of primary stress.

adopt — /ə'dɒpt/

mali — /'mɑ:lɪ/

Examples for secondary stress:

mala fide — /ˌmeɪlə' fɑɪdɪ/

Punjab — /ˌpʌn'dʒɑ:b/

Addition of prefix or suffix normally changes the position of a stress in word.

However the following inflextional suffixes and derivational suffixes do not normally affect the accent.

-ed, -ing, -es, -age, -ance, -er, -ess, -en, -hood, -ice, -ful, -ish, -ly, -less, -ive, -ness, -ment, -ship, -or, -ter, -zen.

EXERCISES

I. What are the two types of stresses in English ? How is it marked ? Give one example for each.

Ans:

II. State if the primary stress marked in the first column is changed when suffix is added as in the second column. If yes, mark it.

/'pæɤeləl/ /pæɤəlelɪŋ/

/pɤə'sɒdɪk/ /pɤəsɒdɪkl/

/ɤɪ'məʊt/ /ɤɪ'məʊtnɪs/

Ans: __________ __________

____

III. Mark the secondary stress in the following words.

(a) /'ɑɪsspa:*/ (b) /pɤɑɪvətɪə*/

(c) /ɤezəlu:ʃn/

Ans: (a) __________ (b) __________

(c) __________

5
Double Pronunciation

Some of the English words possess two types of prounciation. It is because of their two forms ; weak form and strong form. A few of them are given below.

Word	*Weak form*	*Strong Form*
a	/ə/	/eɪ/
am	/əm, m/	/æm/
an	/ən/	/æn/
and	/ənd, nd, ən, n/	•/ænd/
as	/əz/	/æz/
at	/ət/	/æt/
be	/bi/	/bi:/
been	/bi:n/	/bi:n/
but	/bət/	/bʌt/
can	/kən, kn/	/kæn/
could	/kəd/	/kud/
do	/du, də, d/	/du:/
does	/dəz, z, s/	/dʌz/

EXERCISES

I. Write pronunciation of the weak form of the following words.

(a) as (b) be

(c) a (d) can

(e) does.

Ans: (a) __________ (b) __________

(c) __________ (d) __________

(e) __________

II. Write pronunciation of the strong form of the following words.

(a) and (b) am

(c) been (d) but

(e) do

Ans: (a) __________ (b) __________

(c) __________ (d) __________

(e) __________

III. State if the following pronunciation is of weak or strong form.

(a) /æt/ (b) /kud/

(c) /æn/ (d) /kæn/

Ans: (a) __________ (b) __________

(c) __________ (d) __________

Word	*Weak form*	*Strong Form*
for	/fə/	/fɔ:/
from	/frəm/	/frɔm/
had	/həd, əd, d/	/hæd/
has	/həz, əz, z, s/	/hæz/
have	/həv, əv, v/	/hæv/
he	/hɪ, i:, ɪ/	/hi:/
her	/hə, ə:, ə/	/hə:/
him	/ɪm/	/hɪm/
his	/ɪz/	/hɪz/
is	/z, s/	/ɪz/
me	/mi/	/mi:/
not	/nt, n/	/nɔt/
of	/əv, v, ə/	/ɔv/
shall	/ʃel, ʃl/	/ʃæl/
she	/ʃɪ/	/ʃi:/

EXERCISES

I. Write pronunciation of the weak form of the following.

(a) have (b) her

(c) his (d) for

(e) not

Ans: (a) __________ (b) __________

(c) __________ (d) __________

(e) __________

II. Write pronunciation of the strong form of the following.

(a) had (b) have

(c) is (d) me

(e) of (f) from.

Ans: (a) __________ (b) __________

(c) __________ (d) __________

(e) __________ (f) __________

III. State if the following pronunciations are of weak or strong form.

(a) /əv/ (b) /n/

(c) /əd/ (d) /fɔ:/

Ans: (a) __________ (b) __________

(c) __________ (d) __________

Word	*Weak form*	*Strong form*
Sir	/sə/	/sə:/
some	/səm, sm/	/sʌm/
than	/ðen, ðn/	/ðæn/
that	/ðet/	/ðæt/
the	/ðɪ, ðə/	/ði:/
there	/ðə/	/ðɛə/
to	/tu/	/tu:/
us	/əs, s/	/ʌs/
was	/wəz/	/wɔs/
we	/wɪ/	/wi:/
were	/wə/	/wə:/
who	/hu, u:, u/	/hu:/
will	/l/	/wɪl/
would	/əd, d/	/wud/
you	/ju/	/ju:/

EXERCISES

I. Write pronunciation of the strong form of the following.

(a) that (b) shall
(c) to (d) we
(e) will (f) would
(g) the (h) some

Ans: (a) __________ (b) __________
(c) __________ (d) __________
(e) __________ (f) __________
(g) __________ (h) __________

II. Write pronunciation of the weak form of the followings.

(a) there (b) sir
(c) than (d) who
(e) you (f) was

Ans: (a)__________ (b) __________
(c) __________ (d) __________
(e) __________ (f) __________

III. State if the following pronunciation are of weak or strong form

(a) /ðet/ (b) /l/
(c) /sə/ (d) /ʃɪ/

Ans: (a) __________ (b) __________
(c) __________ (d) __________

6
Practice

Q. Write phonetic transcription for the following passage.
I may mention, however, that I was none the worse for abstaining from exercise. That was because I had read in book about the benefits of long walks in the open air. As a result of this advice, I had formed a habit of taking walks, which has still remained with me. These walks gave me a fairly hard constitution.

Ans: ɒɪ meɪ ′menʃn, hɒʊ′evə* ðæt aɪ wɒs nʌn ði: wɜ:s fɔ:* əb′stɪnɪng fɤəm ′eksəsɑɪz. ðæt wɒs bɪ′kɒz aɪ hæd ɤed ɪn bʊks ə′baʊt ðɪ: ′benɪfɪts əv lɒŋ wɔ:ks ɪn ði: ′əʊpəm eə*. æs eɪ ɤɪ′zʌlt əv ðɪs əd′vaɪs, ɑɪ hæd fɔ:md eɪ hæbɪt əv tɔ:kɪŋ wɔ:ks, wɪtʃ hæz stɪl ɤɪ′meɪnd wɪð mi:. ði:z wɔ:ks geɪv mi: eɪ ′feəlɪ ′hɑ:dɪlɪ ˌkɒnstɪ ′tju:ʃn.

EXERCISES

I. Write phonetic transcription for the following passage.
While making these researches he was accustomed to spend night after night in a tall tower, gazing at the heavenly bodies through a telescope. His mind was lifted far above the things of this world.

Ans:

II. Write phonetic transcription for the following passage.

When I finally got up to leave, we both knew that a real friendship had been formed. Luz would go out to the stadium the next day trying to beat me if he could. But I knew that he wanted me to do my best-even if that meant my winning.

Ans:

III. Write phonetic transcription for the following passage.

Well, it was early in the year for salmon and it was not on the bill of fare, but I asked the waiter if there was any. Yes, a beautiful Salmon had just come in, it was the first they had had. I ordered it for my guest. The waiter asked her if she would have something while it was being cooked.

PARTS OF SPEECH

CONTENTS

Sl. No.	Chapters	Exercise written date					Marks	Remarks
1.	Nouns							
2.	Verbs							
3.	Adjectives							
4.	Adverbs							
5.	Articles							
6.	Pronouns							
7.	Prepositions							
8.	Interjections							
9.	Conjunctions							

1
Nouns

A noun can be defined as the name of a person, thing, place, condition and idea.

E.g. Suresh, darkness, Delhi, pen.

There are five types of nouns.

(1) Proper Noun

It is the proper name of a person, place or thing.

E.g. African, Dinesh.

(2) Common Noun

It is the common name of a type or kind of things or persons.

E.g. doctor, dog.

(3) Collective Noun

A noun meaning 'a group' is called collective noun.

E.g. flock, team.

(4) Material Noun

A noun showing the name of a material is called material noun.

E.g. iron, aluminium, plastic.

(5) Abstract Noun

It is the noun expressing a quality which we cannot touch or see.

E.g. brightness, death.

EXERCISES

I. Classify the following nouns:

(a) Himalaya (b) pencil
(c) herd (d) cock
(e) king (f) anxiety
(g) English (h) group
(i) paper (j) Shakespeare

Ans: (a) (b)

(c) (d)
(e) (f)
(g) (h)
(i) (j)

II. Suresh says 'river' is a collective noun. But Sumesh says it is a common noun. Who is right? Why?

Ans:

III. Pick out the noun words from the follwing sentences.
(a) His brightness is really a wonder.
(b) All students should read books.

Ans: (a)

(b)

English nouns are four types in gender; feminine, masculine, common and neuter gender.

A noun denotes a male animal or person is called a masculine gender.

E.g. man, dog.

A noun denotes a female animal or person is called feminine gender.

E.g. Queen, bitch

Some nouns do not show whether it is male or female. Those nouns are applicable to either sexes. Such nouns are called common nouns.

E.g. doctor, teacher.

Collective nouns and abstract nouns have no sex. Hence they are called neuter gender.

E.g. darkness, herd.

EXERCISES

I. Find the gender.
(a) mother (b) paper
(c) team (d) lion
(e) pilot

Ans: (a) (b)
(c) (d)
(e)

II. Pick the nouns from the following sentence and mark their gender.
'Mother bought pen, paper and glass for her son'.

Ans:

III. 'The King believed that he was a God'. Use the word 'Queen' instead of 'King'.

Ans:

There are two types of numbers in English:
Singular and plural.
Singular number denotes single person or thing.

E.g. pen, student.
Plural number denotes two or more things, or persons.

E.g. pens, students.
Plural of a singular noun is formed by
Suffixing 's' to the singular form.

E.g. pen + s → pens
book + s → books
Singular nouns ending in –s, –ch (soft), –sh, –z,—x should be suffixed with '–es' to form their plurals.

E.g. box – boxes, glass – glasses, bush – bushes
Final 'y' of the singular noun is changed to 'ies' to form its plural. This is applicable only if the 'y' is preceded by a consonant.

E.g. baby – babies, party – parties
Final 'f' of 'fe' is changed into 'ves' to form its plurals.

E.g. calf – calves, leaf – leaves

EXERCISES

I. Change the following nouns into plurals.

(a) dish (b) wife
(c) potato (d) knife
(e) chair (f) wood.

Ans: (a) (b)
(c) (d)
(e) (f)

II. Change into singular.

(a) branches (b) fishes
(c) lives (d) words
(e) lilies (f) ladies

Ans: (a) (b)
(c) (d)
(e) (f)

III. What is the number (singular/plural) of the noun 'addresses'? Why?

Ans:

IV. Simply note the rules of plural formation that you learned in the last page.

Singular nouns ending in 'y' but not preceded by a consonant should not be changed their 'y' to 'ies' for forming plurals. Mere addition of 's' is enough.

E.g. boy – boys
toy – toys

In compound words, plural formation may be either in the first word or in the second word or in both of them.

E.g. Mother-in-law → Mothers-in-law
General Manager → General Managers
Woman Servant → Women Servants

Some words have their own plurals. They do not comply with above rules. Most of them are foreign words.

E.g.

data	–	datum
larva	–	larvae
formula	–	formulae
oasis	–	oases
medium	–	media
analysis	–	analyses
phenomenon	–	phenomena
vertebra	–	vertebrae
stimulus	–	stimuli
basis	–	bases
thesis	–	theses
radius	–	radii
fungus	–	fungi
axis	–	axes
memorandum	–	memoranda
species	–	species
datum	–	data
curriculum	–	curricula

EXERCISES

I. What is a singular noun? Give two examples other than given in this book.

Ans:

II. Define 'plural' in your own words. Give four examples other than given in this book.

Ans:

III. Write two times all the foreign nouns and their plural forms that you have studied.

Ans:

2
Verbs

A verb is a word indicating an action.

E.g. write, read, walk.

Verbs are broadly classified into two: transitive verb and intransitive verb.

A transitive verb is a verb which has an object.

E.g. Sudheer *played* football.

A verb which has no object is called an intransitive verb.

E.g. The bell is *ringing.*

Verbs which are limited by the number and person are called finite verbs.

E.g. Suresh *reads* a book.

Verbs which are not limited by number and person are called non-finite verbs.

E.g. Suresh wished *to* read a book.

The verb underlined is a non-finite verb. Hence it does not undergo any change.

Non-finites are three of type

(1) Infinitive

E.g. to read, to walk.

(2) The Participle

E.g. reading, walking, taken

(3) The Gerund

E.g. dancing, breaking.

EXERCISES

I. Write any five verbs other than given in this book.

Ans:

II. Give five examples for intransitive verb.

Ans:

III. What is a transitive verb? Give three examples.

Ans:

IV. Write two examples each for finite verb and non-finite verb.

Ans:

V. What is a non-finite verb.

Ans:

Past tense and past participle of a verb is normally formed by adding 'd', 'ed' or 't' to the present tense form.

E.g. work – worked – worked
place – placed – placed
deal – dealt – dealt

Some other verbs do not comply this rule. Such verbs are called strong verbs. Strong verbs can be divided into two groups.

(1) Verbs those past participle is formed by addition of n/ne/en

E.g. arise – arose – arisen
eat – ate – eaten
give – gave – given

(2) Verbs those past and past participle is formed by inflection of vowel in the present form.

E.g. come – came – come
drink – drank – drunk
sing – sang – sung
sit – sat – sat

EXERCISES

I. Write past and past participle forms of the following verbs.

(a) play (b) dance
(c) correct (d) pour
(e) end.

Ans: (a) (b)
(c) (d)
(e)

II. Write the past and past participle forms of the following verbs. Use a good dictionary.

(a) blow (b) forget
(c) rise (d) steal
(e) write (f) find
(g) fight (h) run
(i) stand (j) win

Ans: (a) (b)
(c) (d)
(e) (f)
(g) (h)
(i) (j)

III, Find the present forms of the following past forms. You may use a dictionary.

(a) spat (b) flung
(c) drew (d) rode
(e) fled (f) sat

Ans: (a) (b)
(c) (d)
(e) (f)

IV. Write the other two forms of the following verbs.

(a) lay (b) stick
(c) fed (d) shut
(e) shown

Ans: (a) (b)
(c) (d)
(e)

3
Adjectives

An adjective is a word which qualifies a noun. It shows quality, kind, number, quantity etc. of the noun.

E.g. red paper, bright student.

There are six types of adjectives in English language. They are:

(1) Adjectives of quality.
(2) Adjectives of quantity.
(3) Adjectives of number.
(4) Demonstrative adjectives.
(5) Distributive adjectives.
(6) Interrogative adjectives.

Adjectives of Quality

Adjective which show quality, kind or condition of a noun is called adjectives of quality.

(a) working woman (b) Chinese silk.

Adjectives of Quantity

Adjective of quantity is a word which shows the quantity of a noun.

E.g. (a) enough work (b) many people.

Adjectives of Number

Another type of adjective is 'adjectives of number'. They shows the number of a noun.

E.g. (a) Six men. (b) Final degree.

EXERCISES

I. Pick out all the adjectives in the following sentences.

1. Two men saw my black shirt.
2. She is white in colour.
3. These Chinese shirt is for you.

Ans:

II. What is an adjective? Give two examples.

Ans:

III. Write the adjective forms of the following words. You may use a dictionary.

(a) picture (b) earth
(c) work (d) face
(e) literature

Ans: (a) (b)
(c) (d)
(e)

IV. Give five examples for 'adjectives of quality.'

Ans:

Demonstrative Adjective

Demonstrative adjective is a word which demonstrate a person or thing.

E.g. (a) These are my books. (b) Those pictures are very bad.

Distributive Adjective

Distributive adjectives are words used for referring persons or things singly or as separate groups.

E.g. (a) Each one of you should read this lesson.
(b) Every employee was given the memo.

Interrogative Adjectives

Interrogative adjectives are words which refer questions. Such as what, which etc.

E.g. (a) Whose cow is this?
(b) Which book should we read?

An adjective word possesses three forms;
positive, comparative and superlative.

Comparative and Superlative degree of regular adjectives are formed by adding 'er' and 'est' to the positive forms respectively.

E.g. hard – harder (comparative) – hardest (superlative)
slow – slower (comparative) – slowest (superlative)

EXERCISES

I, Use in sentence.

(a) slower (b) harder

Ans: (a)

(b)

II. Classify the following adjectives.

(a) rolling	(b) two
(c) exhausted	(d) calling
(e) final	(f) many
(g) each	(h) those
(i) what	(j) natural.

Ans:

Adjectives of quality	Adjectives of quantity	Adjectives of number	Demonstrative adjective	Distributive adjective	Interrogative adjective

III. Find the comparative and superlative forms of the following adjectives.

(a) young (b) bright (c) short

Ans: (a) (b) (c)

IV. What is a comparative adjective used for?

Ans:

In some other cases the prefixes 'more' and 'most' are used to the positive degree to make comparative and superlative degrees respectively.

E.g. beautiful – more beautiful – most beautiful

difficult – more difficult – most difficult.

When using comparative degree the comparative word 'than' should be added in the sentence.

E.g. Leela is more beautiful than Suma.

When using superlative degree the article 'the' should be used just before it.

E.g. The most beautiful lady in this country is Rema.

When using the following comparative forms 'to' is normally used instead of 'than'.

Inferior, superior, junior, senior, prior.

E.g. Suresh is superior to Ramesh.

Study the following comparative and superlative forms. They are irregular. Hence they do not comply with the general rules.

for – former – foremost
hind – hinder – hindmost
out – outer – outermost
up – upper – uppermost

EXERCISES

I. Use in sentence.

(a) more beautiful (b) senior
(c) outermost

Ans: (a) (b)
(c)

II. What are the pecularities of the following adjectives (there are two pecularities).

(a) superior (b) prior
(c) junior

Ans:

III. Write three words whose comparative and superlatives are formed by adding 'more' and 'most'. Do not use the examples given in the last page. You may use a dictionary.

Ans:

bad – worse – worst
good – better – best
little – less – least
much – more – most

The following positive degrees have no comparative and superlative forms.

dead, perfect, singular, unique

Learn the difference between the adjectives in each pair given below.

(1) **few/ a few**

few – practically none

a few – a very small number

(2) **farther/ further**

farther – far (it refers distance)

further – additional

(3) **little/ a little**

little – practically nothing.

a little – a very small quantity.

EXERCISES

I. What are the superlative forms of unique, perfect and singular?

Ans:

II. Use in sentence

(a) further/ farther (b) little / a little

Ans:

III. Write down the irregular adjectives that you have learnt.

Ans:

4
Adverbs

Any word which qualifies a verb, an adjective or another adverb is called adverb.

E.g. She ran so speedily.

Radha looked lovingly.

There are three types of adverbs – Simple, Relative and Interrogative. Simple adverbs can be further divided into adverbs of time, adverbs of place, adverbs of quality, adverbs of number, adverbs of degree, adverbs of reason and adverbs of affirmation or negative. Interrogative adverbs are again divided into six types. They are: Interrogative adverbs of time, interrogative adverbs of number, interrogative adverbs of place, interrogative adverbs of manner, interrogative adverbs of quantity and interrogative adverbs of reason. Relative adverbs are the words 'where', 'when' and 'why'.

See the following examples.

(1) Mr. Kesavan was *formerly* our Principal. (adverbs of time)

(2) You must go *forward*. (adverbs of place)

(3) *Firstly*, I must admit that. (adverbs of number)

EXERCISES

I. What is an adverb? Give five examples.

Ans:

II. Use in sentence.

(a) formally (b) cordially

(c) literally (d) morally

(e) speedily

Ans:

(4) I was writing *speedily*. (adverbs of manner/quality)

(5) It is *so* simple. (adverbs of degree/quantity)

(6) *So*, I have given him my book. (adverbs of reason)

(7) I shall *never* do it (adverbs of negation/affirmation)
(8) *When* will you come to my house. (interrogative adverb of time)
(9) *Where* did you put my pen? (interrogative adverb of place)
(10) *How many* pupils are studying in your class. (interrogative adverb of number)
(11) *How* did you prepare this book? (interrogative adverb of manner)
(12) *How much* do this cost? (interrogative adverb of quantity)
(13) *Why do* you go to Delhi? (interrogative adverb of reason)
(14) Do you know her hostel *where* she is staying? (relative adverb)

Adverbs are formed by the following methods.

(1) By suffixing 'ly' to adjective form.

E.g. normally, personally.

EXCERCISE

I Write one example each for the 14 different adverbs given in the book.

Ans:

(2) by suffixing wise/ward (s)

E.g. downwards, onward

(3) by adding a preposition

E.g. a head, beheld

In normal cases comparative and superlative forms are formed by adding 'er' or 'est' to the positive form.

E.g. late – later – latest

Carefully examine the difference between the words in each pair.

(1) before / ago

before – shows points of time.

ago – shows period of time.

E.g. I shall be there before three o'clock.

I was a student of this school three years ago.

(2) so / as

so – used in negative sentences.

as – used in affirmative sentences.

E.g. Raghu is not so bright as Raju.

Raghu is as bright as Raju.

EXERCISES

I. Show the difference between the two words given in each pair. Use them in sentence

(a) as / so (b) ago / before

Ans:

II. Write comparative and superlative degrees of the following adverbs. You may use a dictionary.

(a) soon (b) softly

(c) much (d) well

(e) early

Ans: (a) (b)

(c) (d)

(e)

III. Form adjectives forms of the following adverbs.

(a) finally (b) cordially

Ans: (a) (b)

5
Articles

The three words 'a', 'an', and 'the' are called articles.
Articles are two of type.
(a) Definite article (the)
(b) Indefinite article (a, an)
The article 'the' is used to point out specific person or thing. Hence it is called definite article.

E.g. It is the Principal.

The articles 'a' and 'an' do not indicate a specific person or thing. Hence they are called indefinite articles.
'A' and 'an' shows singularity. It is used in the meaning of 'one'.
The difference between 'a' and 'an' lies in their usage.
'A' is used before a consonant sound whereas 'an' is used before a vowel sound (a, e, i, o, u).

E.g. a pen, a book, a glass of tea.
an elephant, an institution, an orange
Please note that the selection of indefinite article depends on the first sound it follows, NOT the first letter.

EXERCISES

I. Define an indefinite article. Give two examples.

Ans:

II. Supply suitable indefinite articles. You may refer an English pronouncing dictionary for proper pronunciation.
(a) – man (b) – hour
(c) – university

Ans: (a) ____________ (b) ____________
(c) ____________

III. What is the use of indefinite articles? Give one examples each.

Ans:

The followings are the uses of definite article.

1. Before particular person or thing.

E.g. the woman, the book.

2. Before things which are singular in the world/universe.

E.g. the sun, the Himalayas.

3. Before proper nouns when used as common nouns.

E.g. The Kochi is the Arabian Queen.

4. Before the names of famous books.

E.g. the Mahabharatha, the Othello

5. Before names of rivers, seas etc.

E.g. the Nile, the Red Sea.

6. Before the superlative degree of an adjective.

E.g. the longest, the brightest

7. Before later mentioning of names of persons or things that is already mentioned.

E.g. A cat was sitting in my courtyard
When I reached there, on seeing me, *the cat* darted out.

EXERCISES

I. Write the uses of definite article with examples other than given above.

Ans:

6
Prnouns

A pronoun is a word which stands in lieu of a noun. It is used to avoid repetition.

E.g. Raman was a painter. *He* paints high quality pictures.

There are different types of pronouns in English. They are:

(1) Personal pronouns

Personal pronouns are pronouns which are related to first, second and third persons.

Person	Singular			Plural		
	Nominative	Possessive	Objective	Nominative	Possessive	Objective
I	I	my	me	we	our	us
II	you	your	you	you	your	you
III	he she it	his her its	him her it	they they they	their their their	them them them

E.g. Leela is *my* sister.

He is *our* Principal.

(2) Reflexive pronoun

'Self' or 'selves' forms of my, him, her, them and it are called reflexive pronoun.

EXERCISES

I. Write the possessive (singular) and objective (plural) cases of the following pronouns.

(a) you (b) she

(c) it

Ans:

II. Rewrite the passage given below supplying with suitable pronouns.

I was telling Suresh that (I) sister's marriage is on the coming Sunday. (Suresh) was happy to hear it. (Suresh) told (I) that (Suresh) would come with (Suresh's) family to participate in the function.

Ans:

III. What is the personal pronoun?

Ans:

'Self' is added to show singular number and 'selves' is added to show plural number.

I – myself, we – ourselves, you – yourself,

You (plural) — yourselves, he – himself, her – herself, it – itself, they – themselves.

E.g. He did *his* work himself.

They were reading the book *themselves*.

(3) Demonstrative pronouns

Pronouns which used to point out things or persons are called demonstrative pronouns.

They are: this, that, these, those.

E.g. *This* is the house that I built.

I found *those* pictures laying on my table.

(4) Indefenite pronouns

Pronouns which do not refer to any particular person or thing but used as general are called indefinite pronouns. Main indefinite pronouns are: few, many, some, something, all, one, none, nobody, many, anybody and everybody.

E.g. *Few* men were happy.

All people engaged in the work.

EXE RCISES

I. Supply with suitable reflexive pronouns.

(a) Radha washed her clothes.

(b) The elephant pulled the timber.
(c) Suma and Shylaja solved the problem.

Ans: (a)

(b)

(c)

II. Use in sentence.
(a) ourself (b) yourself.

Ans: (a)

(b)

III. Define an indefinite pronoun. Give two examples.
Ans:

IV. What is the possessive form of 'I'?
Ans:

(5) Interrogative pronouns

Pronouns that are used to ask questions are called interrogative pronouns.

They are: who, whose, whom, what, which.

E.g. *Who* did open this door?
What is your name?

(6) Reciprocal pronouns

Reciprocal pronouns are pronouns which shows mutual relationship.

E.g. All of them asked questions *one another*.
The two friends told stories *each other*.

(7) Distributive pronouns

The three words either, neither and each are called distributive pronouns.

E.g. *Each* person know it.
Either sides are false.

EXERCISES

I. What is an interrogative pronoun? Give two examples.
Ans:

II. Use in sentence.

(a) whose (b) which

Ans:

III. Why 'one another' is called a reciprocal pronoun? Give example.

Ans:

IV. Pick out the pronouns.

(a) All pupils should learn what they are told to.

(b) My father is a doctor.

Ans:

(8) Relative pronouns

Pronouns which relates one clause to another is called relative pronouns.

They are: who, which, what, that, but, as.

E.g. This is the house *that* I built.

This is the man *who* is going to win the election.

The relative pronouns 'who' has two other forms.

whose – possessive

whom – objective

Though the meaning of the relative pronouns 'that' and 'which' are same, that is used to relate persons and things whereas which is used to relate animals and inanimate things.

In some cases the relative pronoun may be omitted.

E.g. It is the man (whom) I met yesterday.

Study the books (which) I supplied.

EXERCISES

I. Classify the following pronouns.

(a) they (b) my

(c) which (d) whose

(e) each (f) each other

(g) either (i) all

(j) this (k) herself

(l) ourselves (m) whom.

Ans:

II. Use in sentence.
(a) Which (as relative pronoun)
(b) What (as relative pronoun)

Ans:

7
Prepositions

Preposition is a word or group of words which connects words in a sentence.

E.g. I found him *in* trouble.

I am going *to* college.

The important prepositions in English are:

on, in, at, up, off, between, under, as, into, onto, by, for, of, with, about etc.

When mentioning time 'at' is used before a point of time (***E.g.*** at 5 o'clock) 'on' is used before days and dates (***E.g.*** on Monday) and 'in' before years, month and age (***E.g.*** in 1999).

When mentioning places 'at' is used before exact place, street etc. (***E.g.*** at Edapal) 'in' is used before city, state and country (***E.g.*** in India).

'on' also means 'above' when used before a thing, particular place etc. (***E.g.*** on the floor). 'To' denotes direction, destination etc. (***E.g.*** to school) 'up' means 'from a lower position to higher position (***E.g.*** climb up).

EXERCISES

I. Write the meaning of

(a) with (b) in

(c) of (d) at

Ans: (a) (b)

(c) (d)

II. Use in sentence

(a) off (b) by

(c) about

Ans: (a)

(b)

(c)

III. Use correct prepositions.

(a) He is a man ______ principles.
(b) I enjoy fly ______ the air.
(c) Please make him free ______ the jail.
(d) The monkey climbed ______ the tree.
(e) The pen is ______ the table.
(f) Fish is ______ the pond.
(g) School is situated ______ the post office and the bank.

Ans: (a) (b)
(c) (d)
(e) (f)
(g)

'Off' means away from (*E.g.* please go off)'into' denotes a motion to a point within (*E.g.* the stone went into the pond). 'Onto' denotes a motion 'to the top of' (*E.g.* cat jumped onto the table). 'By' means 'near' 'along' and 'during' (*E.g.* He passed by the post office). 'For' indicates 'because of' 'towards', 'in favour of', and 'directed to' (E.g. I am working for money). 'Of' shows possessiveness (*E.g.* four (legs of the cow). 'With' means 'through', 'by means of', 'in company of' and 'in relation to' (*E.g.* She goes to school with her mother). 'Between' means 'in the middle of two objects or persons' (*E.g.* I am between devil and deep sea). 'About' means 'near', 'round' and 'concerning' (*E.g.* what is your opinion about songs?).

EXERCISES

1. Write examples for the following usages of prepositions.

(a) Into ______ a motion to a point within.
(b) by ______ in the meaning of 'along'.
(c) for ______ in the meaning of 'because of'.
(d) with ______ in the meaning of 'through'.
(e) about ______ in the meaning of 'round'.

Ans: (a)

(b)

(c)

(d)

(e)

In addition to the above mentioned rules some preopositions are used alongwith particular words. As they are part and parcel of the words, they should be followed when using such words. A few of them are given below.

accuse of
admit to/of
agree to/with/upon
appeal to
appoint to
arrive at
believe in
boast of
busy with
comply with
contrary to
deal in/ with
differ from
disagree with
envious of
excuse for
free from
glad of
hand over
hide from
ignorant of
indebted to
inform of
inquire of
invited to
knock at
last for
laugh at
lead to
long for
married to
moved by
occur to
open to
partial to
pass for
popular with
pride in
proud of
quick of
quick at
refer to
relieve at
reply on
repent of
repulation for
sensitive to
stoop to
subscribe to
taste for
true to
victim of
zest for

EXCERCISE

I. Write appropriate prepositions for the words given below. You may refer to dictionary or grammar book.

Ans:

(a) aquainted – (a)
(b) aim – (b)
(c) allude – (c)
(d) bestow – (d)

(e) brood	–	(e)
(f) compete	–	(f)
(g) deviate	–	(g)
(h) eligible	–	(h)
(i) fond	–	(i)
(j) gifted	–	(j)
(k) heir	–	(k)
(l) insist	–	(l)
(m) meddle	–	(m)
(n) name	–	(n)
(o) opposed	–	(o)
(p) preside	–	(p)
(q) remarkable	–	(q)
(r) suitable	–	(r)
(s) thankful	–	(s)
(t) used	–	(t)
(u) yield	–	(u)

8
Interjections

Interjections are meaningless words which is uttered when a person get excited with over joy, sorrow, fear or surprise.

Important interjections in English are:

Ha, Alas, Hello, Hush, Oh, Ah, Hurrah, Good gracious, Good heaven, Ah me etc.

E.g. Hush! they are coming.

Hurrah! I have succeeded in the examination.

Oh! it is a pity.

Alas! I have lost my leg.

The pecularity of interjections are

(a) They do not possess any meaning but strong emotion.

(b) They are not connected with the rest of the words in a sentence.

(c) It has no other forms.

EXERCISES

I. What are the pecularities of interjections ?

Ans:

II. Use in sentence.

(a) Ah (b) Hello

(c) Oh

Ans: (a)

(b)

(c)

(d)

III. What is an interjection ?

Ans:

9
Conjunctions

Conjunctions are words which joints sentences or words together, which, where, and, but, whom, whose, what, as though, as soon as, as well as, even if, not only .... but also, so that, or, still, yet, while, where as, either .... or, neither .... nor, since, that, if etc. are the main conjunctions in English.

E.g. I drank a glass of water <u>and</u> ate a piece of bread.

There are three types of conjunctions.

The conjunction which connects two independent clauses are called co-ordinating conjunction.

E.g. Go and fetch a note book *or* come with me.

The conjunction which connects a noun or adverb clause to some other clause is called a subordinating conjunction.

E.g. I believe *that* he is not bright.

The conjunctions which are in pairs are called relating conjuctions.

E.g. Suresh *not only* ate a mango *but also* ate an apple.

EXERCISES

I. What are the three types of conjunctions? Give examples for each other than given above.

Ans:

II. Use in sentence

(a) but (b) and

(c) or (d) that

Ans:

(a)

(b)

(c)

(d)

HOME STUDY SERIES - 3

SENTENCES AND SPOKEN ENGLISH

P. V. GOPALAKRISHNAN

SENTENCES

CONTENTS

Sl. No.	Chapter	Exercise written date									Marks	Remarks
1.	The Sentence											
2.	Subject-Predicate											
3.	Phrases											
4.	Kinds of Clauses											
5.	Noun Clause											
6.	Adjective Clause											
7.	Adverb Clause											
8.	Kinds of Sentences											
9.	Simple Sentence											
10.	Compound Sentence											
11.	Complex Sentence											
12.	Compound Complex Sentence											
13.	Transformation											

1
The Sentence

A sentence is a group of words which expresses a complete sense.

E.g. She is very beautiful.
The cow is eating.

Sentence can be broadly classified into four groups. They are:

(1) Declarative or Assertive Sentence

This kind of sentence expresses a statement or fact. They declare or assert a fact. Hence they are called so,

E.g. It is good.
Leela has passed.

(2) Imperative Sentence

Imperative kind of sentences express request, wish or command.

E.g. Please come with me.
May the God bless you!
Go and fetch your books.

EXERCISES

I What is a sentence? Give two examples other than given above.

Ans:

II. State whether the following groups of words make sentences or not.

	Ans:
1. I do my.	1. ________
2. Who is this?	2. ________
3. Please make a.	3. ________

III. What is an imperative sentence? Give two examples other than given on the last page.

Ans:

IV. What is an assertive sentence? Give two examples.

Ans:

(3) Exclamatory Sentence

An exclamatory sentence expresses a strong feeling of wonder, sorrow or gratitude. Exclamation mark, not period, is given at the end of such sentences.

E.g. How beautiful she is !
What a death it is !
How kind of you !

(4) Interrogative Sentence

This type of sentence shows a question. Such type of sentences are used to ask questions. Question (interrogation) mark is used at the end of such sentences.

E.g. Who is coming?
What is your problem?

WORD ORDER

Word order in the above four types of sentences are quite different. Hence it is very important to know the word order of each. In declarative sentences, the word order is as follows.

Noun/pronoun + verb + object + ___________

E.g. He is my brother.

In imperative sentences the subject (the first noun or pronoun) is often omitted and the verb comes first. It is followed by the rest of the sentence.

E.g. Shut the door.

In exclamatory sentences, the sentence starts with an exclamatory word. The sentence often ends with an auxiliary verb such as 'is, am or are.'

E.g. What a beautiful sight it is !

In interrogative sentences, the word order is:

Question word + auxiliary verb + noun/pronoun + ___________

E.g. What do you know?
Whose is this pen?

2
Subject-Predicate

A sentence can be divided into two main parts; subject part and predicate part. A subject is a word (normally it is either a noun or a pronoun) about which something is given in the sentence. Look at the sentence given below.

Mohan is an intelligent boy.

In the above sentence the noun 'Mohan' is the subject because about whom the rest of the sentence is telling. A subject normally comes at the beginning of the sentence. The subject word and the other words related to it together are called the subject part of the sentence.

Predicate part of a sentence is the words in a sentence which does not include in the subject part.

Mohan	is an intelligent boy.
Subject	Predicate

Look at the above sentence. The words other than 'Man' makes the predicate part because it tells about the subject. From this, it is clear that words which tell something about the subject is called the predicate.

In the imperative sentences the subject is often omitted and in the interrogative sentences the subject is placed in the centre of the sentence.

EXERCISES

I. What is an exclamatory sentence? Give two examples.

Ans: 1.

2.

II. State whether the following sentences are true or false.

	Ans:
(1) Why you do know that?	(1) ________
(2) The book you read.	(2) ________
(3) How wonderful is it !	(3) ________

III. Correct the following sentences.

	Ans:
(1) She my wife is.	(1) ________
(2) Whom you do know?	(2) ________

IV. What is an interrogative sentence? Give two examples other than given in this book.

Ans:

V. What is a predicate? Give two examples.

Ans:

VI. What is a subject? Give two examples.

Ans:

VII. Mark subject and predicate parts in the following sentences.

(1) They are travelling.

(2) The mother and her two sons are waiting outside.

(3) All the students in the class may leave the school.

(4) What shall I do?

(5) Shut the doors.

(6) I shall come with you.

3
Phrases

A phrase is a group of words that make an incomplete sense. Though it makes a sense, it cannot stand alone as an independent sentence.

E.g. At last, she left the house.

The underlined two words together make a phrase. The most important pecularity of a phrase is that it has no subject or predicate part. These types of phrases can be added to a sentence as prefix or sufix irrespective of the kind of sentence.

CLAUSES

A clause is a group of words which make a complete sense. Though it can make a complete sense, it is often treated as a part of sentence because it is not enough to be considered as a sentence. The fact is that it can make sense but it has no features of a sentence. Some times it can be treated as a small sentence having its own subject and predicate.

E.g. The man in the hall is my father.

In the above example the underlined words make a sense, hence they are called a clause.

EXERCISES

I. What is a clause? Give one example other than given in this book.

Ans:

II. What is a phrase? Give one example other than given in this book.

Ans:

III. Mark phrase and clause in the following sentences.

(1) I shall give you commission at the rate of fifty percentage.
(2) By two o'clock I shall be at your house.
(3) I met a man whom I saw yesterday.
(4) I do not care what they can do.
(5) The students who were obedient, were admitted to the class.

4
Kind of Clauses

As said earlier, clauses are groups of words which give a complete sense and form part of a larger sentence. They are used in a sentence to make the sentence larger and more meaningful.

clauses can be divided into three groups.

(1) Noun clause

(2) Adjective clause

(3) Adverb clause

In the noun clause, there will be a subject and predicate. They do the function of a noun in a sentence.

E.g. The man who won the prize is coming.

An adjective clause is a group of words which do the function of an adjective.

E.g. This is a dog which has large jaw.

An adverb clause is a group of words which do the function of an adverb.

E.g. The thief ran when he saw the police coming.

EXCERCISES

I. What are the subdivisions of clauses?

Ans:

II. What is an adjective clause? Give two examples other than given above.

Ans:

III. What is an adverb clause? Give two examples other than given in this book.

Ans:

IV. What is a noun clause? Give two examples other than given in this book.

Ans:

5
Noun Clause

Noun clause is, as stated earlier, a group of words which do the function of a noun in a sentence.

A noun clause, in elaborate sense, can do several functions in a sentence. The different functions of noun clauses are given below.

(1) Subject of a verb.

E.g. How he can do this is a question.
Whatever he had done is correct.

(2) object of a verb.

E.g. No one knows what I think.
Do what you like.

(3) Nominative.

E.g. I don't care, whoever you are.
I call you thief, whatever your name is.

(4) object of a preposition.

E.g. She talked me about what her brother said.
You will get a reward for what you have done.

(5) Complement of a verb.

E.g. Her brother is like what I said.
It feels like what he described.

EXERCISES:

I. What is a noun clause? Give two examples.

Ans:

II. What are the uses of a noun clause. Give two examples for each other than given above.

Ans:

6
Adjective Clause

The adjective clause is to perform the duty of an adjective. Though it is a group of words it does the duty of an adjective. For introducing an adjective clause relative pronoun or relative adverb is always used. However, in some rare cases the introductory word is omitted.

E.g. That man <u>who was my brother</u> is a thief.
This is the ground <u>where I played in my youth</u>.
Bring books <u>I need</u>.

EXERCISES

I. What is the difference between a noun clause and an adjective clause?

Ans:

II. Give two examples for adjective clause.

Ans: (1)

(2)

III. State whether the following sentences contain noun clause or adjective clause.

(1) That is the dog which bit me.

Ans: __________

(2) My brother brought what I asked.

Ans: __________

(3) My brother, who a serious man, not fit to this job.

Ans: __________

(4) Those persons who are coming are my workers.

Ans: __________

7
Adverb Clause

An Adverb clause is a group of words which do the function of an adverb in a sentence.

There are different kinds of adverb clauses.

Importants of them are:

(1) **Adverb clause of time**

Adverb clause of time gives a time reference. In such clauses, the introductory words are as, before, when, after, since, till, whenever etc.

E.g. When the train came, we all got in.
Since the arrival of English men, English schools were established.

(2) **Adverb clause of place**

This clause locate a thing or person. Introductory word 'where' or 'wherever' is also used.

E.g. I met the principal, where I found him yesterday.
Take your wife wherever you go.

(3) **Adverb clause of cause**

This clause is used to show the cause for the matter described in the main clause. Introductory words 'because, as, since, that' etc are also used.

E.g. He failed in the examination because he had studied nothing.
As he had studied nothing, he failed in the examination.

(4) **Adverb clause of purpose**

This clause expresse the purpose of the matter shown in the main clause. Introductory words such as that, so that, in order that etc. are used at the beginning of the clause.

E.g. She worked hard that her husband might get good treatment.
Suresh studied well so that he might get through the examination.

(5) **Adverb clause of manner**

This clause is used to expresses how the idea expressed in the main clause occurred. Introductory words such as if, as, as though etc. are used at the beginning of this clause.

E.g. He walks as if he were tired.
Students sit in the class as though they understood the lecturing.

(6) **Adverb clause of condition**

Adverb clause of condition expresses on which condition the idea expressed in the main clause occurrs. Introductory words are unless, if, provided, whether etc. are used.

E.g. If you come, I shall be happy.

This certificate will be incomplete, unless it bears chancellor's signature.

EXERCISES

I. What is an adverb clause?

Ans:

II. Write the subdivisions of adverb clause. Give one example for each other than given in this chapter.

Ans:

8
Kinds of Sentences

We have seen earlier that sentences can be broadly classified into four main groups considering their nature. They are assertive, imperative, exclamatory and interrogative sentences.

In this section we are dealing with another type of classification based on the structure of sentences.

According to this kind of classification, sentences can be classified into four main groups such as:

(1) Simple sentence.

(2) Compound sentence.

(3) Complex sentence.

and

(4) Compound complex sentence.

A simple sentence carries only one subject and one predicate. A compound sentence carries two or more independent clauses. A complex sentence carries one principle clause and one or more subordinate clause(s). A compound complex sentence is a combination of two or more co-ordinate clauses and one or more subordinate clauses. Detailed analysis of each is given in the following chapters.

EXERCISES

I. What are the subdivisions of sentences based on structure?

Ans:

II. What are the subdivisions of sentences based on nature?

Ans:

III. What is the structural pecularity of a compound sentence?

Ans:

IV. What is the structural pecularity of a compound complex sentence?

Ans:

9
Simple Sentence

A simple sentence is a meaningful group of words which has only one subject and one predicate.

E.g. Leela reads
S S

The cow in the field makes loud noise
S P

The subject part is the group of words which is consisted of a noun, pronoun, gerund, to infinitive or an adjective used as a noun and the attributes related to the subject word.

E.g. To err is human. (to infinitive)
S P

He is rich. (pronoun)
S P

Smoking is injurious to health. (gerund)
S P

Suresh is going to school. (noun)
S P

Besides the mentioned subject word, there may or may not be attributes in the subject part.

EXERCISES

I. What is a simple sentence?

Ans:

II. Write two examples for sentences having a pronoun subject.

Ans: (1)

(2)

III. Write two examples for sentences having a gerund subject.

Ans: (1)

(2)

IV. Write two examples for sentences having a infinitive subject.

Ans: (1)

(2)

Given below are different types of attributes.

Article, adjective, to infinitive, adjectival phrase, reflexive pronoun, noun/phrase in apposition and possessive form of a noun.

E.g. *A* man (S) is sitting in the room. (P) (article)

A *white* man (S) is flying in the sky. (P) (adjective)

Bird's beak (S) touched his head. (P) (possessive)

He *himself* (S) did his work. (P) (reflexive pronoun)

His brother, *a neat man,* (S) is her husband. (P) (adjective phrase)

To go home (S) is his aim. (P) (to infinitive)

Suresh, *the manager of the firm,* (S) declared that he sould resign. (P)

(noun/phrase in opposition)

EXERCISES

I. What are the different types of attributes?

Ans:

II. Write two examples for sentences having possessive attribute.

Ans: (1)

(2)

III. Write two examples for sentences having adjectival attribute.

Ans: (1)

(2)

IV. Write two examples for sentences having article attribute.

Ans:

The main word of the predicate part is the verb. It is further modified by adverbial qualifiers such as adverb, participle or to infinitive.

E.g. He (S) ran *fastly.* (P) (adverb)

He (S) left the room *smiling.* (P) participle)

She (S) asked *to leave.* (P) (to infinitive)

In addition to verb and its qualifier there will be object if the verb is in transitive, in the predicate part.

E.g. She (S) reads *a book.* (P) (object)

Objects can be in the form of noun, to infinitive, pronoun, gerund, phrase etc.

She (S) reads *a book.* (P) (noun)

She (S) saw *him.* (P) (pronoun)

She (S) wishes *reading.* (P) (gerund)

She (S) wished *to leave.* (P) (to infinitive)

EXERCISES

I. Write two examples for sentences having a noun-object.

Ans:

II. Write two examples for sentences having adverbial qualifier.

Ans: (1)

(2)

III Write two examples for sentences having a gerund-object.

Ans: (1)

(2)

IV. Write two examples for sentences having a noun-object.

In a simple sentence, there may be two objects. One is direct object and the other is indirect object.

Direct objcct is the word which gets as the answer of the question that has the following structure.

To whom + verb of the sentence.

E.g. Leela gave me (indirect object) an apple. (direct object)

Normally indirect object is placed first and direct object thereafter.

Given below are two tables showing analysis of subject part and predicate part of the sentence given below.

The white man in the chair is giving his children advice.

Subject: The white man in the chair

Article	Adjective	Noun	Prepositional Phrase
The	white	man	in the chair

Predicate: is giving his children advice.

Verb	Direct Object	Indirect Object
is giving	advice	his children

EXERCISES

I. What is a direct object? Give two examples.

Ans:

II. What is an indirect object? Give two examples.

Ans:

III. Correct the followings

(1) Suresh gave a pen his sister.

(2) He bought a shirt his son.

Ans: 1.

2.

IV. Analyse the following sentences.

(1) The black dog in the street is taking its child home.

(2) She fed her children with food.

Ans:

In some cases the sentence will be incomplete in meaning without a particular word though it contains a verb.

Ram appeared happy.

In the above sentence the meaning will be incomplete without the word 'happy'. Such words that are added to an incomplete predication is called complements. When it qualifies the subject, it is called subject complement and when it qualifies the object, it is called object complement.

The following tables describe the position of both subject complement.

Subject		Predicate		
Attribute	Subject	Verb	Object	Object Complement
The	man	forced	him	to sign

Subject		Predicate	
Attribute	Subject word	Verb	Subject complement
The aged	man	is	kind.

EXERCISES

I. What is a complement? Give two examples.

Ans:

II. What is a subject complement? Give two examples.

Ans:

III. What is an object complement? Give two examples.

Ans:

IV. Analyse the answers of exercise II and III.

Ans:

10
Compound Sentence

Compound sentence is a sentence of a combination of two or more independent clauses. Each clause has its own meaning and they can stand alone.

These independent clauses are joined together by a conjunction to make compound sentence.

E.g. I read a book and my brother wrote a letter.

Look at the above sentence. It can be divided into two sentences by simply omitting the conjunction 'and' and putting a period in the place of conjunction omitted.

The conjunctions such as still, and, but, yet, for, or etc. are used to connect independent clauses together.

A mere comma can do the work of a conjunction in some rare cases.

E.g. I came, I saw, I conquered.

EXERCISES

I. What is a compound sentence? Give two examples.

Ans:

II. How can a compound sentence divide into two or more sentences.

Ans:

III. Use in sentences

(a) but (b) or (c) still

Ans: (a)

(b)

(c)

11
Complex Sentence

A complex sentence is a combination of a principal clause and one or more subordinate clause(s).

The subordinate clause supports or describes elaborately the principal clause. Hence it may be a noun clause, adjective clause or adverb clause.

Look at the example given below.

When my uncle reached home, I gave him the book, which he always wished to read.

In the above sentence 'I gave him the book' is the principal clause and 'when my uncle reached home' and 'which he always wished to read' are the two subordinate clauses.

Look at another example.

I told him that he should come tomorrow.

In this sentence 'I told him' is the principal clause and 'that he should come tomorrow' is the subordinate clause.

EXCERCISES

I. What is a complex sentence? Give two examples.

Ans:

II. **Find principal clause and subordinate clause(s) of the following sentences.**

1. When the mind gets absorbed in sushupti or deep sleep, we do not experience the phenomenon of a world and the like.
2. When that child was about to be killed, he cried out loudly and very bitterly for fear of death.
3. Verily yoga is not possible for him who eats too much, nor for him who fasts excessively, nor for him, who is addicted to too much sleep or keep vigil too long.

Ans:

12
Compound Complex Sentence

Compound complex sentences are a combination of both compound and complex. Hence in it, we can see two or more coordinate clauses and one or more subordinate clause(s).

Look at the examples given below.

1. *When I heard a noise, I ran to my house and shut the doors.*
2. *As I am the principal of this college, I have the right to suspend you from the college and ask you not to enter the campus.*

In the first sentence 'when I heard a noise' is the principal clause and 'I ran to my house' and 'shut the doors' are the two coordinate clauses.

In the second sentence 'As I am the principal of this college' is the subordinate clause and 'I have the right to suspend you from the college' and 'ask you not to enter the campus' are the two co-ordinate clauses.

EXERCISES

I. What is a compound complex sentence? Give two examples.

Ans:

II. What are the structural difference between compound-simple, complex-simple and compound complex-simple sentences.

Ans:

13
Transformation

Simple Into Compound

Simple sentence has only one subject and one predicate. But compound sentence must have atleast two coordinate clauses.

If it is the matter how can one simple sentence convert to a compound sentence?

It is not a difficult work.

If you have a logic mind and a little practice, you can easily do it.

In a simple sentence that is given for conversion, there may be a participal phrase or a noun phrase that can be expanded into a clause.

Some essential words, according to your taste should also be added to expand that phrase into a clause. See the example given below.

Doing the business, he became rich.

In this sentence 'he became rich' is a clause. But 'doing the business' is a participal phrase. You can develop it into 'he did the business'. Then join the two clauses using the coordinate conjunction 'and'. Then you will get a sentence as given below.

He did the business and he became rich.

EXERCISES

I. How can a simple sentence change into a compound sentence?

Ans:

II. Change the following sentences into compound.

1. Being a rich man, he bought a car.
2. Working in the field, he got tired.
3. Writing well, he became famous.
4. Reading the news paper, he got angry.
5. Being an advocate, he argued his own case.

Ans:

Compound Into Simple

If you could get a thorough idea about converting simple into compound, conversion of compound into simple will be very easy. Because you may apply the opposite principle you have studied in the last chapter.

As a simple sentence contains only one subject and one predicate, you have to change one clause of the compound sentence into a participal phrase or noun phrase. Put a comma after it and write the coordinate clause after it.

E.g. I am a kind man and I showed him enough mercy. (compound)
Being a kind man, I showed him enough mercy. (simple)

In the first sentence 'I am a kind man' is a clause. It is changed into a participal construction such as 'being a kind man'. This clears the matter and the sentence becomes compound when adding this phrase with the other clause.

EXERCISES

I. How can a compound sentence change into simple. Give two examples.

Ans:

II. Change the following sentences into simple.
(1) He is a player. He won name and fame.
(2) I worked hard. I got enough money to buy a car.
(3) She thought. She found a way.

Ans:

Simple Into Complex

Converting simple sentence into complex sentences is also simple, if you have acquired a little technical aspects of the clauses.

Conversion can be done by expanding a word or phrase into a clause. Expansion may be done to noun clause and adjective clause (mostly using relative pronoun) and adverb clause using phrasal construction.

E.g. She loves an Englishman (simple)
She loves a man who is English (complex)

In the first sentence, there is only one subject and a predicate. From that the words 'an Englishman' is expanded to a subordinate clause and attached to the main clause. The principal clause stood unchanged.

See another example.
They appreciated my speech (simple)
They appreciated what I spoke (complex)

The words 'my speech' is expanded to 'what I spoke' which is a subordinate clause.

EXERCISES

I. How can a simple sentence change into complex. Give one example.

Ans:

II. Change the following sentences into complex.

1. She is a beautiful girl.
2. They are good at work.
3. The cow is white.
4. Her brother is a decent man.
5. He is fast in speech.

Ans:

Complex Into Simple

Conversion of complex sentence into simple can be done by using the reverse principle of conversion of simple sentence into complex sentence.

What we have done in converting a simple sentence into a complex sentence is expanding a word or phrase into a clause.

Do the very opposite of this i.e. reduce a clause into a word or phrase.

Look at the example given below.

Ask her when shall we meet again. (complex)

Ask her the time of our next meeting. (simple)

In the first sentence subordinate clause 'when shall we meet again' is reduced into the phrase 'the time of our next meeting'.

See another example.

Jawahar Lal Nehru who was the Prime Minister of India was an intelligent man. (complex)

Jawahar Lal Nehru, the Prime Minister of India, was an intelligent man. (simple)

The clause 'who was the Prime Minister of India' in the first sentence is reduced into a phrase and used as apposition in the second sentence to make it simple.

EXERCISES

I. How can a complex sentence change into a simple sentence? Give one example.

Ans:

II. Change the following sentences into simple.

1. The students stopped playing cards, when the teacher came in.
2. When I was a boy, I was a little naughty.
3. Deers ran away when they heard lion's roar.

Ans:

SPOKEN ENGLISH

CONTENTS

Sl. No.	Chapter	Exercise written date									Marks	Remarks
		I	II	III	IV	V	VI	VII	VIII	IX		
1.	What is Spoken English											
2.	Pecularities of Spoken English											
3.	Expressions											
4.	Situational Conversations											

1
What is Spoken English?

English language has two sides as all the other languages have except, some dead languages. Those two sides are 'Written English' and 'Spoken English'.

A language lives on the lips of the people. Though the written language has many advantages over the spoken one, spoken language is the life sap of all languages.

English has many varieties such as American English, Australian English, British English, Scotish English, Indian English etc. In which British English (both spoken and written) especially Oxford English is considered the standard English.

Among the different varieties of English, Indian English is less different from British English. Its vocabulary, spelling and grammer are exactly the very same with that of the standard English. But pronunciation differs a little.

Spoken form of the language is the most important form because it is used for direct communication. Hence a little knowledge of it is essential to everybody. This section is a venture to depict some short cut methods for acquiring some knowledge on spoken English.

EXERCISES

I. What is the true varieties of English?

Ans:

II. What is the pecularity of Indian English?

Ans:

III. What are the two sides of a language?

Ans:

IV. What is the advantage of spoken English over written English?

Ans:

2

Pecularities of Spoken English

Given below are some pecularities of spoken English, study them carefully and try to construct simple speeches complying with those rules.

(1) One important pecularity of spoken English is preposition in an interrogative sentence moves to the end of the sentence.

E.g. Whom you are waiting for?
What do you think of?

(2) Pronouns possess two types of possessives such as:
I — my, mine
We — us, ours
You — your, yours
They — their, theirs

The second possessive forms given in the above list is mostly associated with spoken form.

E.g. This is mine.
Which is yours?

When using such possessive forms, place them at the end of a sentence.

(3) In spoken English 'going to' construction is often used to indicate simple future or strong intention.

E.g. I am going to see a cinema.
I am going to resign.

(4) In a conversation between two parties, there may be questions and answers. It is found in many parts of the world a tendency to avoid repetition of the matters while answering.

E.g. Do you know this man?
Yes, I do.

In the above sentences, the answer sentence should be like this; 'Yes, I know this man'. But it is reduced to 'Yes, I do'. From that the person who asked the question gets a clear idea of what the answer intended. Such a reduction saves time and labour. So it is common in spoken English.

(5) Another feature of spoken English is abbreviated forms. In spoken English most of the usages have abbreviated form. A few are given below with their expanded form.

I am — I'm
I have — I've
I will — I'll
I would, I had — I'd
you are — you're
you have — you've
you will — you'll
you would, you had — you'd
he is, he has — he's
he would, he had — he'd
he will — he'll
she is, she has — she's
she would, she had — she'd
she will — she'll
it has, it is — it's
it would, it had — it'd
we are — we're
we will — we'll
we have — we've
we would, we had — we'd
they are — they're
they will — they'll
they have — they've
they would, they had — they'd
there is, there has — there's
there will — there'll
can not —can't
could not — could'nt
do not — don't
does not — doesn't
did not — didn't
have not — haven't
has not — hasn't
had not — hadn't
is not — isn't
might not — mightn't
must not — mustn't
need not — needn't
ought not — oughtn't
shall not — shalln't

should not — shouldn't
was not — wasn't
were not — weren't
will not — won't
would not — wouldn't

(6) Inversion of words in a sentence is very common in spoken English.

E.g. Rajan has done, I know that what I said.
This is an inverted sentence. Its actual form is 'I know that Rajan has done what I said'. The inversion was done for getting emphasis on the last part of the inverted sentence.

(7) The 'why not' construction is used in spoken language to ask questions. It is the short form of 'why + should + (subject) + not'. It should be noted that no pronoun or noun comes after 'why not'.

E.g. Why not come with me?
Why not join the army?

(8) In spoken English word 'stress' is very familiar. Stress is the extra force used for the pronunciation of a particular syllable in a word.

E.g. fif<u>teen</u>.
<u>horse</u>-box
In each of the above given examples, the underlined syllables are stressed syllables. Hence extra force should be given to those syllable while pronouncing them.

(9) Intonation is the rise and fall of voice in a spoken sentence. As it has the power to change the nature of a sentence, it is commonly used in the spoken language.

E.g. You are <u>Going</u>?
If the rise of voice is not given to the last part of the sentence, it would be an assertive sentence. But this type of intonation changed its nature and now it is a question.

EXERCISES

I. What is 'going to' construction used for?

Ans:

II. Write the two possessive forms of the following pronouns.

	Ans:
(1) you	(1) ________ ________
(2) they	(2) ________ ________
(3) we	(3) ________ ________

III. Give two examples for avoiding repetition in spoken form.

Ans:

IV. Give two examples for inversion of words in spoken form.

Ans:

V. Write contracted form of the followings.

	Ans:
(1) she has	(1) __________
(2) we are	(2) __________
(3) I will	(3) __________
(4) will not	(4) __________
(5) might not	(5) __________
(6) they would	(6) __________

IV. Write expanded form of the followings.

	Ans:
(1) shouldn't	(1) __________
(2) don't	(2) __________
(3) there's	(3) __________
(4) he'd	(4) __________
(5) you've	(5) __________
(6) I'm	(6) __________
(7) we'll	(7) __________

VII. What is a stress? Give three examples.

Ans:

VIII. What is intonation? Give two examples.

Ans:

IX. What is the expanded form of 'why not ....' construction?

Ans:

3
Expressions

Expressing gratitude

Spoken form has its own style and usage. If you want to express your gratitude, one of the following expression may be used.

Thanks.
Thanks a lot.
Thanks very much.
Thank you.
Thank you very much.
Many thanks.
It is very nice of you.
It is very kind of you.
Grateful to you.
I am thankful to you.

Response to an expression of gratitude

In response to an expression of gratitude the following expressions are found to be used.

Welcome.
You are welcome.
Okay (ok)
That's all right.
Not at all.
It's a pleasure.
Don't mention it.
Please don't mention.

Expressing wonder

Wonder may be expressed in different ways according to the taste of the speaker.

However a few expressions are very common in spoken English. They are:

Beautiful!
Wonderful!

How wonderful!
Fantastic!
Smashing!
Stunning!
My goodness!
O boy!
How sweet a voice!
What a wonderful............!
What a terrible............!
What a smart............!
What a beautiful............!
What a lovely............!

Expressing wish

When one meets with another the first words uttered will be that of wish. There are a variety of expressions used for wishing a man. Given below are a few of them.

Good morning.
Good afternoon.
Good evening.
Good night.
How do you do.
How are you?
Hello.

Reply to the above expressions are given below, carefully study them.

Good morning → Good morning.
Good afternoon → Good afternoon.
Good evening → Good evening.
Good night → Good night.
How do you do → How do you do.
How are you? → I am fine.
Hello → Hello.

Asking opinion

If you want to know another person's opinion, you may use following expressions at the beginning of sentences.

What's your opinion of............
Do you agree with............
What do you think of............

What are your views about............
Are you in favour of............
What do you say about............
Express your views on............

Expressing opinion

When you are asked to express your opinion about a matter, you may use one of the following expressions at the beginning of your reply.

I'd say............
I believe............
I think............
I suppose............
I feel............
In my opinion............
It seems to me............
As far as I'm concerned............
As far as I can see............
I'm convinced............
I'm strongly persuaded............
I'd just like to say that............
I would like to say............
I am afraid to say that............

Expressing agreement

The following expressions are used to show agreement.

I agree.
I agree entirely.
I couldn't agree more.
Quite.
Exactly.
That's right.
Of course.
Sure
By all means
I'd be glad to ......

Expressing disagreement

Above mentioned expressions are for agreement. But if you disagree with a point one of the following expressions should be used.

I'm not so sure.
But don't you think............
Well, I think............
............but on the other hand............

Do you really think so?
I don't agree.
I disagree.
I am sorry, but............
I really can't agree because............
I'd like to say yes, but............

Expressing past habit

For expressing past habit the following methods are used.

(1) By using would + bare infinitive

E.g. I would read novel in the night.

(2) By using the word 'used to'

E.g. I used to read novel in the night.

(3) By using past simple.

E.g. I read novel in the night.

(4) By using the phrase 'was in the habit of'.

E.g. I was in the habit of reading novel in the night.

Asking for information

Particular question words are used to get particular information. Given below are a few question words and corresponding information it convey. Auxiliary verb will change according to the tense.

(a) *time*: When did............

E.g. When did she found me?

(b) *manner*: How do............

E.g. How do you go home?

(c) *place*: Where do............

E.g. Where do you go?

(d) *number*: How many............

E.g. How many students have passed?

(e) *quantity*: How much............

E.g. How much is the amount?

(f) *choice*: which............

E.g. Which house do you like ?

(g) *distance*: How far............

E.g. How far is your house from the temple?

(h) *reason*: Why were............

E.g. Why were you report the matter?

(i) *duration*: How long............

E.g. How long did you wait for me?

(j) *price*: what is............

E.g. What is the price of this pen?

(k) *frequency*: How often............

E.g. How often you go abroad?

Polite question forms

For asking polite questions, there are a few expressions. They are:

could you kindly............

would you please............

I wonder if you would............

I wonder if you could............

I would like to............

Expressing manners

Terms of manners are very few in number. If it is added to the beginning of the sentence, it would please the hearer. Given below are terms of manners.

Please............

Excuse me,............

Pardon me,............

Allow me............

I am very happy to............

Would you please............

I am afraid to............

EXERCISE

I. Complete the following conversation.

Raju: Good morning John,

John: ....

Raju: ....?

John: I am going to the post office.

Raju: .... for me?

John: Sure.

Raju: Thank you, John.

John: ....

II. Complete the following conversation.

Mohan: Hello, Sunil........................ yesterday?

Sunil: I went for a film, you know.

Mohan: ....?

Sunil: At "the Globe".

Mohan: ....?

Sunil: "Gandhi"

Mohan: Well,..........................?

Sunil: Oh! it's really wonderful ....?

Mohan: No. I haven't, I've been too busy. You see. Would you like to see it again?

Sunil: ....

Mohan: Then shall we go together tonight.

Sunil: ....

II. Complete the following conversation meaning fully.

Grand son: Do you find life boring, grand pa?

Grand pa: ...., I still find it interesting.

Grand son: ....?

Grand pa: I have a lot of hobbies, dear.

Grand son: ....

Grand pa: Reading, gardening, painting ....

Grand son: Did you do these even in your younger days?

Grand pa: ....; I would water the plants in the morning. In the evening I would do a lot of reading.

Grand son: So you spend your time profitably,..........................?

Grand pa: ....

IV. Complete the following conversation.

Rahim: Good morning, Ram

Ram: ....?

Rahim: I want to reach the office early today.

Ram: ....?

Rahim: Today is independence day. I want to hoist the flag.

Ram: Oh! I forgot it. If so I should also be in hurry.

Rahim: Then O.K. see.

Ram: ....

V. Complete the following conversation.

Dileep: Excuse me. What is the price of this pen?

Shop keeper: ....

Dileep: ....

Shop keeper: There are other models, Sir. A pen like this has many good qualities. Hence this high cost.

Dileep: ....

Shop keeper: Oh, sure. Here is brown coloured.

Dileep: ....?

Shop keeper: Ten rupees. Do you want any other things?

Dileep: ....

4

Situational Conversations

At An Office

Consumer: Excuse me, could you tell me the postage for this envelope.

Counter Clerk: Oh, sure, wait one minute. ....Fifteen rupees.

Consumer: Thank you, will it reach the address tomorrow?

Counter Clerk: No. It would take two days.

Consumer: Two days! I don't think I have much time.

Counter Clerk: Then you can send it by Speed Post.

Consumer: Where is the Speed Post counter? What are the formalities?

Counter Clerk: Please go to Counter No. 14. He will help you.

Consumer: Thank you. You are very helpful.

Counter Clerk: No mention. It is our duty.

Over Telephone

"Hello, is it the police station?"

"Yes, who is calling?"

"This is the manager of Paradise Hotel, sir."

"Yes, what is the problem there?"

"Sir, I doubt something. One man in the Room No. 13 of our hotel is mysterious. I doubt he is a thief."

"What is his name? Which address he has given you?"

"He says his name is Raju, Sir. I don't think so. He is, I doubt, a Muslim, Sir."

"Then we shall come there. Don't let him leave your hotel. We shall reach in five minutes. Thank you for your information."

"It's OK Sir. We shall keep him."

At the Hospital

Doctor: Yes, come in .... sit down please. What is your problem?

Patient: I have headache, doctor.

Doctor: Is it sever? When did it start?

Patient: It is very sever. It started a week ago, I applied pain balm. But it did not cure.

Doctor: Have you any other discomforts such as fever, vomitting tendency etc.

Patient: Nothing, Sir.

Doctor: Then lie down please. Take deep breath.

Patient: What is the matter with me, Sir? Is it anything serious?

Doctor: No.............no.............no. Why do you fear so much? It is a very simple matter. I shall prescribe one tablet. It would clear the matter.

Patient: Thank you Sir. What is your consultation fees?

Doctor: It is 50 rupees.

Patient: Thank you Sir.

Meeting with a Friend

Ramesh: Good morning Raju.

Raju: Good morning. Where are you going?

Ramesh: I am going to the city market. Where do you go?

Raju: I am going to see a cinema. Why do you go to the city market?

Ramesh: I want to buy some vegetables and fruits.

Raju: I heard apples are very cheap now-a-days. Is it true?

Ramesh: Yes, apples are very cheap now.

Raju: How much is the cost of it per kilogram?

Ramesh: A kilogram of apple cost Rs.5.

Raju: Then I shall come with you. I also want two kilograms of apple.

Ramesh: OK. Let us move.

At the Bus Station

Chandran: From where shall I get the bus to Bangalore?

Staff: You will get bus from the northern side of the bus station.

Chandran: How often there is bus to Bangalore?

Staff: There is bus to Bangalore in every half an hour.

Chandran: How much is the ticket price?

Staff: Ticket charge is 150 rupees.

Chandran: When shall I reach there if I get the next bus?

Staff: You will reach at 2 O'clock.

Chandran: Thank you for your information. Give me one Bangalore ticket.

Staff: Here is the ticket, Sir.

Chandran: Thanks.

EXERCISES

I. You have been waiting at the bus station for a very long time. But you don't get the bus to your village or town. Meanwhile you meet a friend of yours. Construct a short dialogue between you and your friend.

Ans:

II. Imagine that your gold chain has been stolen. You went to the police station for lodging a complaint. Write a dialogue between you and the sub-inspector of police.

Ans:

III. You have met one of your friend in the street. Write an imaginary conversation between yours and your friend.

Ans:

IV. Imagine thwat you are at the railway station. Write a dialogue between you and the railway staff.

Ans:

V. Imagine that you have gone to a hospital. Write a conversation between you and the doctor.

Ans:

VI. Write a conversation between you and your father on the occassion of your sucess of examination.

Ans:

HOME STUDY SERIES - 4

TENSES AND GRAMMAR

P. V. GOPALAKRISHNAN

TENSES

CONTENTS

Sl. No.	Chapters	Exercise written date					Marks	Remarks
1.	Time							
2.	Present Simple (form)							
3.	Present Simple (uses)							
4.	Present Continuous (form)							
5.	Present Continuous (uses)							
6.	Present Perfect (form)							
7.	Present Perfect (uses)							
8.	Present Perfect Continuous (form)							
9.	Past Simple (form)							
10.	Past Simple (uses)							
11.	Past Continuous (form)							
12.	Past Continuous (uses)							
13.	Past Perfect (form)							
14.	Past Perfect (uses)							
15.	Past Perfect Continuous (form)							
16.	Past Perfect Continuous (uses)							

CONTENTS

Sl. No.	Chapters	Exercise written date					Marks	Remarks
17.	Comparison							
18.	Future Simple (form)							
19.	Future Simple (uses)							
20.	Future Continuous (form)							
21.	Future Continuous uses)							
22.	Future Perfect (form)							
23.	Future Perfect (uses)							
24.	Future Perfect Continuous (form)							
25.	Future Perfect Continuous (uses)							

1
Time

In English time is broadly divided into three . Each one of these three is further divided into four. See the chart given below.

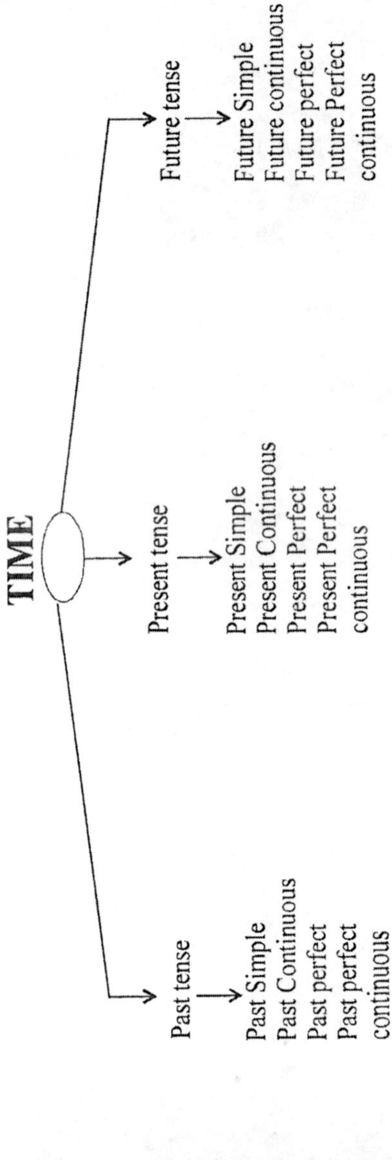

NB: In some grammar texts the word 'progressive' is used instead of 'Continuous'.

EXERCISES

I. What are the three main tense forms in English?

Ans:

II. How is future tense further classified?

Ans:

III. What are the sub-divisions of present tense?

Ans:

IV. What are the sub-divisions of past tense?

Ans:

2

Present Simple (Form)

Present simple form of a verb is the base form or dictionary form of that verb.

E.g. I *learn* English.

You *go* home.

Here 'learn' and 'go' are base forms or dictionary forms.

If the subject of a sentence is in the third person singular, '–s' or '–es' should be added to the base form.

E.g. He reads a novel.

Suma goes to school.

The pronouns 'he,' 'she', 'it' and all singular proper nouns are in the third person singular. '–es' is added only if the verb ends in s, sh, ch, ss, o. In all the other cases '–s' is enough.

E.g. go – goes, dance – dances

Final 'y' is changed to 'ies',

E.g. study – studies.

In some other cases present simple form of verb is expressed in another way. It is 'do + base form'. In such cases 'does + base form' makes the present simple form of verb having a third person singular subject.

EXERCISES

I. Write present simple form of the following verbs.

(a) worked (b) supplied (c) singing.

Ans: (a) ______ (b) ______ (c) ______

II. Pick out the third person singular words from the following groups.

(a) Rajeev (b) I (c) me

(d) he (e) Radha (f) you.

Ans: (a) ______ (b) ______ (c) ______

(d) ______ (e) ______ (f) ______

III. Frame two present simple sentences using the following group of words.

I, she, novel, paper, read, reads.

(1)

(2)

IV. When should 'es' is added to the present simple form of verbs. Give two examples.

Ans:

Negative form of present simple is:

do/does + not + base form.

E.g. I do not read novels.
He does not read novels.
Interrogative form of present simple is as follows:
do/does + subject + base form + ...

E.g. You speak so speedily → Do you speak so speedily?
She dances → Does she dance?
Negative interrogative of the present simple is formed as follows:
do/does + subject + not + ...

E.g. You speak so speedily → Do you not speak so speedily?
She dances → Does she not dance?
There is a slight veriation in the word order if the negative interrogative is in contracted form.

E.g. You speak so speedily → Don't you speak so speedily?
She dances → Don't you dance?

EXERCISES

I. Change the following sentences into present simple negative form.
(a) I am going to school.
(b) She comes to school.

Ans:

(a)

(b)

II. Frame questions from the following sentences.
(a) You speak truth.
(b) I write an article.

Ans:

(a)

(b)

III. Change the following sentences into negative interrogatives.
(a) I know English.
(b) She writes Hindi.

Ans:

(a)

(b)

IV. Write interrogative negative (contracted) form of the following sentences.

(a) I know her.

Ans: (a)

3
Present Simple (Uses)

1. Present simple is used to show a habitual action.

E.g. I often go to my uncle's house.

She always drinks coffee.

In showing habitual action, an adverb or adverb phrase such as often, always, never, everytime, usually etc. are used.

2. It is used to show an universal truth.

E.g. The sun rises in the east

One and one makes two.

3. Present simple is used in quotations.

E.g. Radha said "I and my husband are going to Delhi."

4. It is used to show a planned future activity.

E.g. I attend the function tomorrow.

5. This tense form is used with verbs of perception, even though it is continuous process at the time of speaking.

E.g. I hear a sound from outside.

6. It is used with the exclamatory sentences starting with 'here' or 'there.'

E.g. Here she comes!

EXERCISES

I. State whether the following sentences are correct.

(a) Mr. Chopra never reading novel.

(b) I am seeing an air-bus in the sky.

(c) The cow is giving us milk.

Ans: (a)

(b)

(c)

II. What are the uses of present simple. Give one example for each.

Ans:

4
Present Continuous (Form)

Present Continuous form of the verb is: is/am/are + ing form of the verb.

E.g. Sudha is reading a newspaper.
I am going to college.
The auxiliary verb 'am' is used only if the subject is 'I'.
Auxiliary verb 'is' is used when the subject is third person singular (he, she, it, all singular names).
Auxiliary verb 'are' is used when the subject is 'you' and 'third person plural'.
Negative form of the present continuous tense is formed by adding 'not' after the auxiliary.

E.g. Sudha is not reading a newspaper.
I am not going to sleep.
Interrogative form of this tense is formed by the inversion of the subject and the auxiliary.

E.g. Is Sudha reading a newspaper?
Am I going to college?
Negative interrogative is formed by adding not to the interrogative form after the subject.

E.g. Is Sudha not reading a newspaper?
Am I not going to college?
Contracted form of the negative interrogation is quite different in word order. In such sentences contracted form of 'not' is added to the auxiliary.

E.g. Am n't I going to college?
Is n't Sudha reading a newspaper?

EXERCISES

I. Write five present continuous sentences using the following words.

Subject	Verb	Object
I	go	Delhi
She	read	novel
Radha	play	tennis
You	write	article
They	complete work	

Ans:

II. Change the above sentences into negative interrogatives?

Ans:

5
Present Continuous (Uses)

1. The main use of the present continuous tense is that it expresses an action what is happening at the time of speaking.

E.g. Ram is drinking a glass of milk.
They are playing football.

2. It is used to express a frequent action.

E.g. It is always raining.
Radha is always playing chess.

3. It is also used to indicate an immediate future activity.

E.g. Who is coming tomorrow?
I am leaving tomorrow.
In this context, future time should be mentioned.

EXERCISES

I. Rewrite the following sentences using appropriate form (present simple/present continuous) of the verbs given in brackets.

(a) They (intend) to go abroad tomorrow.
(b) Savitri (sing) a song.
(c) Ram and Radha (dance).

Ans: (a)
(b)
(c)

II. Change the following sentences into interrogative sentences.

(a) I am going to school.
(b) Radha is playing tennis.
(c) They are completing their work.

Ans: (a)
(b)
(c)

III. Change the answers of exercise II into negative interrogative (contracted) sentences.

Ans: (a)
(b)
(c)

6
Present Perfect (Form)

Present perfect form of the verb is: have/has + the past participle form of the verb.

E.g. I have seen her.

She has met her husband.

The auxiliary very 'has' is used only if the subject is in third person singular. 'Have' is used on all other cases. Past participle form of the regular verb is formed by '–d' or '–ed' to its present form.

Negative form of present perfect is formed by putting 'not' after the auxiliary.

E.g. I have not seen her.

She has not met her husband ?

Interrogative of the present perfect is formed by inverting the auxiliary and the subject.

E.g. Have I seen her?

Has she met her husband.

Negative interrogative is formed by putting 'not' after the subject in the interrogative form of this tense form.

E.g. Have I not seen her?

Has she not met her husband?

Negative interrogative (contracted) form is formed by putting contracted form of negative after the auxiliary in the interrogative form of this tense.

E.g. Haven't I seen her?

Hasn't she not met her husband?

EXERCISES

I. Find the tense form of the following sentences.

(a) Raveendran is swimming in the pond.

(b) Moon revolves round the earth.

(c) Who has done this?

Ans: (a)

(b)

(c)

II. Change the following sentences into negative interrogative form.

(a) My son has painted a picture.

(b) Suma has just completed dancing.

(c) I have passed S.S.L.C. examination.

Ans: (a)

(b)

(c)

III. Change the answers of Exercise II into contracted form of negative interrogative.

Ans: (a)

(b)

(c)

7

Present Perfect (Uses)

1. This tense form is used to express an action just completed.

E.g. I have just seen a cinema.
She has just completed her work.
Note: Time reference should not be added in this tense form.

2. It is also used to express an action completed in the past when the speaker wishes it to be presented as just completed.

E.g. I have seen Ooty.
I have read Hamlet.

3. This tense form is used to show a past action of which effect is still in action.

E.g. He has passed B.A. degree.
I have got an award.

EXERCISES

I. Change the following sentences into negative.
(a) Who has tore my book?
(b) Have I seen you yesterday?
(c) I have just finished my work.

Ans: (a)

(b)

(c)

II. What are the uses of present perfect? Give one example for each.

Ans:

8

Present Perfect Continuous (form)

Present perfect continuous tense is formed by the following formula.
have/has + been + ing form of the verb.
'Has' is used only if the subject is in third person singular. But on all other cases 'have' is used.

E.g. I have been waiting for you since 8 o'clock.
She has been studying Sanskrit since passing matriculation.

Negative of this tense is formed by putting 'not' after the auxiliary (and before the word 'been').

E.g. I have not been waiting for you.
She has not been studying Sanskrit.

Interrogative of this tense is formed by inverting the auxiliary and the subject.

E.g. Have I been waiting for you?
Has she been studying Sanskrit?

Negative interrogative is formed by putting the negative word 'not' after the subject in the interrogative sentences.

E.g. Have I not been waiting for you?
Has she not been studying Sanskrit?

EXERCISES

I. Change the following sentences into present perfect continuous.
(a) I have studied English.
(b) Rama has done her home work.
(c) They have played cricket.

Ans: (a)

(b)

(c)

II. Change the answers of exercise I into interrogatives.

Ans: (a)

(b)

(c)

III. Change the answers of exercise I into negative interrogatives.

Ans: (a)

(b)

(c)

Negative interrogative (contracted form) is made by adding 'n' t' to the auxiliary in the interrogative form.

E.g. Have't I been waiting for you?

Hasn't she been studying Sanskrit?

Present perfect continuous is used to show an action started in the past but still continuing.

E.g. I have been waiting for you since 8 o'clock.

It has been raining since this morning.

Note:

Always care not to identify this tense with present perfect in usage. Present perfect is used to show an action completed in the past. But present perfect continuous is used to show an action started in the past and still continuing.

EXERCISES

I. Change the answers of exercise I in the iast 'exercises page' into negative.

Ans: (a)

(b)

(c)

II. Correct the followings, if they are incorrect.

(a) I have seen her yesterday.

(b) The baby has cried since last night.

(c) Leela has been not learning English.

(d) Haven't completed you the work?

(e) Ram has been taught Hindi for four years?

Ans: (a)

(b)

(c)

(d)

(e)

9
Past Simple (Form)

Past simple tense is formed by adding '–ed' to the base form of verb, if the verb is regular verb. In irregular verbs the past simple form is formed by inflecting the vowel in the verb.

E.g. I wrote a letter yesterday.
Sheela completed her home work at 5 o'clock.
Negative form of this tense is made by splitting the verb into 'did + present form' and adding 'not' after 'did'.

E.g. I did not write a letter yesterday.
Sheela did not complete her homework at 5 o'clock.
Interrogative form of past tense is formed by the following formula.
did + subject + base form of the verb + ...

E.g. Did I wrote a letter yesterday?
Did Sheela complete her homework at 5 o'clock?
Negative interrogative form is formed by adding 'not' after the subject in the interrogative sentence.

E.g. Did I not write a letter yesterday?
Did Sheela not complete her homework at 5 o'clock?
Negative (contracted) interrogative form is made by adding contracted form of 'not' after the word 'did' in the interrogative sentences.

E.g. Didn't I write a letter yesterday?
Didn't Sheela complete her homework at 5 o'clock?

EXERCISES

I. Write three sentences as examples of past simple tense.

Ans: (a)
(b)
(c)

II. Change the answers of exercise I into interrogative form.

Ans: (a)
(b)
(c)

III. Change the answers of exercise II into interrogative negative form.

Ans: (a)

(b)

(c)

IV. Change the answers of exercise II into negative form.

Ans: (a)

(b)

(c)

10
Past Simple (Uses)

1. Past simple is used to express an action completed at a certain time in the past.

E.g. Sheela saw a picture two days ago.
Raman met me yesterday.
In such a condition, past time reference should be added.

2. It is used also to show a period of action completed in the past.

E.g. I studied in that college for three years.
Kala worked in the Canara Bank for two years.

3. It is used to show a past habit.

E.g. I often drank brandy.
He always wrote articles.

Note:

'Used to + base form of verb' is also used to show past habit.

E.g. I used to drink brandy
He used to write articles.

EXERCISES

I. Change the following sentences into 'used to' construction.

(a) Leela often visited her uncle.
(b) Chief Minister of our state always went to court.
(c) Our dog always barked at strangers.

Ans: (a)
(b)
(c)

II. What are the uses of past simple? Give one example for each.

Ans:

11
Past Continuous (form)

Past continuous tense form is as follows:

was/were + 'ing' form of verb.

The auxiliary 'was' is used only if the subject is 'I' and third person singular. In all the other cases 'were' is used.

E.g. Rajan was sleeping.
They were playing.

Negative is formed by putting 'not' after the auxiliary.

E.g. Rajan was not sleeping.
They were not playing.

Interrogative is formed by using the auxiliary before the subject.

E.g. Was Rajan sleeping?
Were they playing?

Interrogative negative is formed by putting 'not' after the subject in the interrogative sentence.

E.g. Was Rajan not sleeping?
Were they not playing?

Interrogative negative (contracted) is formed by adding contracted form of 'not' to the auxiliary in the interrogative sentence.

E.g. Wasn't Rajan sleeping?
Weren't they playing?

EXERCISES

I. Change the following sentences into past continuous.
(a) I am writing a letter.
(b) They have finished writing examination.
(c) Rajan slept for a long period.

Ans: (a)
(b)
(c)

II. Change the answers of exercise I into interrogative form.

Ans: (a)
(b)
(c)

III. Change the answers of exercise II into negative interrogatives.

Ans:

(a)

(b)

(c)

12

Past Continuous (Uses)

1. Past continuous tense is used to express a past activity which were continued for a certain period in the past. It should be followed by a time reference.

E.g. I was reading the paper in the morning.
Rema was painting a picture yesterday.

2. It is used instead of present continuous in indirect speech.

E.g. Raman said "I am not singing." (direct)
Raman said that he was not singing. (indirect)

3. Past continuous tense is used to express two past parallel activities in progress.

E.g. I was playing with my friend when my mother called me.
While I was playing, it started raining.

EXERCISES

I. Find the tense form of the following sentences.
(a) Birds have been singing.
(b) Birds have sang.
(c) Birds sing.

Ans: (a)
(b)
(c)

II. State if the following sentences are correct.
(a) God have guiding us.
(b) Cow are giving us milk.

Ans: (a)
(b)

III. Correct the following sentences.
(a) Are not Suresh reading?
(b) I have not written a letter yesterday.

Ans: (a)
(b)

13
Past Perfect (Form)

Past perfect tense form is as follows:
had + past participle of verb.

E.g. Meera had sung a song.
I had seen Delhi.
Negative of past perfect tense is formed by putting 'not' after the auxiliary.

E.g. Meera had not sung a song.
I had not seen Delhi.
Interrogative of past perfect is formed by inverting subject and auxiliary.

E.g. Had Meera sung a song?
Had I seen Delhi?
Negative interrogative is formed by adding 'not' after the interrogative sentence.

E.g. Had Meera not sung a song?
Had I not seen Delhi?
Negative interrogative (contracted) form of past perfect tense is formed by adding contracted form of 'not' after the auxiliary in the interrogative sentence.

E.g. Hadn't Meera sung a song?
Hadn't I seen Delhi?

EXERCISES

I. Change the following sentences into past perfect.
(a) Dinesh and his friends played football.
(b) They are preparing.
(c) I have read a novel.

Ans: (a)
(b)
(c)

II. Change the answers of exercise I into negative form.

Ans: (a)

(b)

(c)

III. Change the answers of exercise II into interrogatives.

Ans: (a)

(b)

(c)

14
Past Perfect (Uses)

1. It is used to express an activity completed before a point of time in the past.

E.g. When I reached there, he had drank milk.
By 6 o'clock the theatre had closed.

2. It is used in indirect speech instead of present perfect tense in the direct speech.

E.g. Suma said "I have passed the examination." (direct)
Suma said that she had passed the examination. (indirect)

3. When two actions are mentioned in the past, the first action should be in the past perfect and the later in past simple.

E.g. We all had slept deeply and took bath.
After he had fought well, he stopped it.

4. It is used to show a past wish unfulfilled.

E.g. I wish I had a car.

EXERCISES

I. Correct the following sentences.
(a) They said that they have won the match.
(b) I wish I have a motorcycle.
(c) When he came, his father have left the house.

Ans: (a)
(b)
(c)

II. Change the answers of exercise I into interrogative form.

Ans: (a)
(b)
(c)

III. What are the uses of past perfect?

Ans:

15
Past Perfect Continuous (Form)

The form of past perfect continuous tense is: had been + 'ing' form of the verb.

E.g. They had been working in the field.
Krishna had been composing a music.
Interrogative form of the past perfect continuous tense is formed by inverting the subject and auxiliary.

E.g. Had they been working in the field?
Had Krishna been composing a music?
Negative form of this tense is formed by putting 'not' after the auxiliary.

E.g. They had not been working in the field.
Krishna had not been composing a music.
Negative interrogative form is formed by putting 'not' after the subject in the interrogative sentence.

E.g. Had they not been working in the field?
Had Krishna not been composing a music?
Negative interrogative (contracted) is formed by putting contracted form of 'not' after the auxiliary in the interrogative sentence.

E.g. Hadn't they been working in the field?
Hadn't Krishna been composing a music?

EXERCISES

I. Write three examples of past perfect continuous.

Ans: (a)
(b)
(c)

II. Change the answers of exercise I into negatives.

Ans: (a)
b)
(c)

III. Change the answers of exercise II into interrogatives.

Ans: (a)

(b)

(c)

IV. Change the answers of exercise III into negatives.

Ans: (a)

(b)

(c)

16

Past Perfect Continuous (Uses)

This tense form is used to express an activity which were continued for a certain period in the past. This is always followed or preceded by another action.

E.g. They had been working in the field before went to cinema.
Krishna had been composing a music before read the novel.

EXERCISES

I. What is the use of past perfect continuous? Give two examples other than the two given above.

Ans:

II. Change the following sentences into negative interrogatives (contracted).

(a) Ajit had been studying for M.A. degree.
(b) They had been dancing.
(c) Mr. Pradeep had been building a house.

Ans: (a)
(b)
(c)

III. Correct the following sentences.

(a) Had not they singing a song?
(b) Harish had been submitted his thesis.

Ans: (a)
(b)

IV. Rewrite the following sentences using correct tense forms of the verbs given in brackets.

(a) Mr. Lalu (read) before (drink) alcohol.

(b) I (see) a bird in the sky.

(c) The cow (run) in the morning.

Ans: (a)

(b)

(c)

17
Comparison

[Present perfect — present perfect continuous — past simple — past perfect — past perfect continuous.]

Present perfect tense is used to express a just completed action.

Present perfect continuous is used to show an activity started in the past but still continuing.

Past simple is used to express an action completed at a certain time in the past.

Past perfect is used to express an activity completed before a point of time in the past.

Past perfect continuous is used to express an activity which were continued for a certain period in the past.

The difference can be seen clearly in the following diagram.

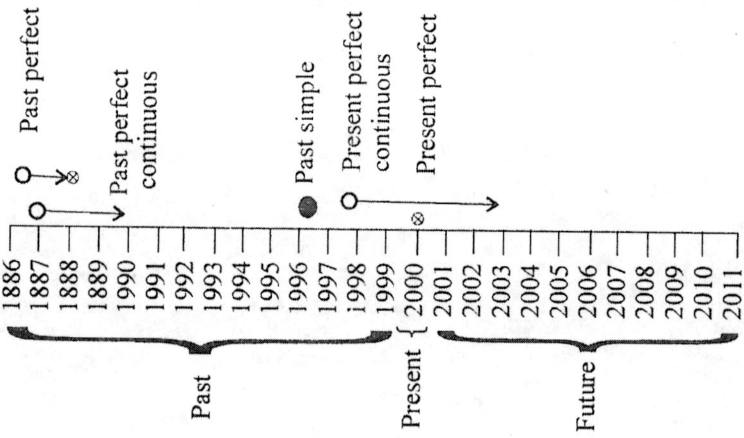

EXERCISES

I. What is the main difference between the following sentences.

(a) I have seen a cinema.

(b) I saw a cinema.

Ans:

II. What is the difference between present perfect continuous and present perfect.

Ans:

III. Change the following ideas into suitable sentences.

(a) Rajan studied English from 1991 to 1993. This is the year 1999.

(b) Rajan started learning music two years ago. He is still studying music.

Ans: (a)

(b)

18
Future Simple (Form)

'Shall/will + base form of the verb' is the form of future simple tense.

'Shall' is normally used with first person (singular and plural). 'will' is used with all other subjects.

E.g. I shall see him.
He will see him.

Negative form of this tense is formed by putting 'not' after shall/will.

E.g. I shall not see him.
He will not see him.

Interrogative is formed by inverting the subject and 'shall/will'.

E.g. Shall I see him?
Will he see me?

Interrogative negative is formed by adding 'not' after the subject in the interrogative sentence.

E.g. Shall I not see him?
Will he not see me?

Interrogative negative (contracted) form is formed by putting contracted form of 'not' after 'shall/will' in the interrogative sentences.

E.g. Shalln't I see him?
Won't he see him?

Note: Contracted form of 'will not' and 'shall not' are won't and shan't respectively.

EXERCISES

I. Change the following sentences into future simple.
(a) I am going to see a cinema.
(b) He has worked.
(c) You are dancing.

Ans: (a)
(b)
(c)

II. Change the answers of exercise I into interrogative form.

Ans: (a)

(b)

(c)

III. Change the answers of exercise II into negative.

Ans: (a)

(b)

(c)

19
Future Simple (Uses)

It is used to show a pure future activity. There will be no personal elements.

E.g. The school will re-open on the next Monday.
The road will remain closed tomorrow.

Note: Near future, intention, and pre-fixed activity in the future are not expressed using future simple tense. For showing them 'going to' construction is always used.

E.g. I am going to take a ticket.
The university is going to publish the examination results.

EXERCISES

I. What is the use of future simple? Give one example.

Ans:

II. Change the following sentences into 'going to' construction.
(a) Soman will book a ticket.
(b) Seema will depart to Mumbai.
(c) I shall pass the examination.

Ans: (a)
(b)
(c)

III. What is the difference between the sentences given in the exercise II and your answers to that.

Ans:

20
Future Continuous (Form)

Future continuous tense is formed by the following way.

Shall be/will be + 'ing' form of the verb. 'Shall be' is used with 'first person' and 'will be' is used with second person and third person.

E.g. I shall be learning English the next year.

He will be coming with me for the next month's programme.

Negative of future continuous is formed by adding 'not' after 'shall/will'.

E.g. I shall not learning English the next year.

He will not be coming with me for the next month's programme.

Interrogative of this tense is formed by inverting shall/will and the subject.

E.g. Shall I be learning English the next year?

Will he be coming with me for the next month's programme.

Negative interrogative is formed by putting 'not' after the subject in the interrogative sentence.

E.g. Shall I not be learning English the next year.

Will he not be coming with me for the next month's programme.

Negative interrogative (contracted) is formed by putting contracted form of 'not' after 'shall/will' in the interrogative sentence.

E.g. Shan't I not be learning English the next year?

Won't he be coming with me for the next month's programme.

EXERCISES

I. Write three examples for future continuous.

Ans: (a)

(b)

(c)

II. Change the answers of exercise I into negative.

Ans: (a)

(b)

(c)

III. Change the answers of exercise I into interrogative.

Ans: (a)

(b)

(c)

IV. Change the answers of exercise III into negative interrogative.

Ans: (a)

(b)

(c)

21

Future Continuous (Uses)

1. This tense form is used to express a future continuous activity.

E.g. I shall be going to Chennai tomorrow.
He will be coming tomorrow.

2. It is used also not as a continuous activity but an incident naturally occuring action.

E.g. He will be seeing Rajan.

EXERCISES

I. Change the following sentences into future continuous.

(a) She will learn music.
(b) She was continuing her study.
(c) Leela is playing chess.
(d) Rajeev plays football.

Ans: (a)
(b)
(c)
(d)

II. What is the difference between simple future and future continuous.

Ans:

III. Write three sentences having the use shown in the note no. 2.

Ans: (a)
(b)
(c)

IV. What are the uses of future continuous? Give three examples.

Ans: (a)
(b)
(c)

22
Future Perfect (Form)

The form of future perfect is:

Shall/will + have + past participle form of the verb.

'Shall' is used with first person and 'will' is used with second person and third person.

E.g. Sheela will have completed writing examination by 4 o'clock.
I shall have done it by tomorrow.

Negative of future perfect is formed by adding 'not' after the auxiliary.

E.g. Sheela will not have completed writing examination by 4 o'clock.
I shall not have done it by tomorrow.

Interrogative is formed by inverting auxiliary and subject.

E.g. Will Sheela have completed writing examination by 4 o'clock ?
Shall I have done it by tomorrow?

Negative interrogative is formed by putting 'not' after the subject in the interrogative sentence. Its contracted form is formed by adding 'n't' to the subject in interrogative sentence.

E.g. Will Sheela not completed writing examination by 4 o'clock?
Shan't I have done it by tomorrow?

EXERCISES

I. Write three sentences as examples for future continuous.

Ans:

(a)

(b)

(c)

II. Change the answers of exercise I into negative.

Ans: (a)

(b)

(c)

III. Change the answers of exercise I into interrogative.

Ans: (a)

(b)

(c)

IV. Change the answers of exercise III into negative.

Ans: (a)

(b)

(c)

23
Future Perfect (Use)

This tense form is used to express a future activity which will be completed by a certain time.

Note: When using time clause in showing a future activity, please not to use future perfect but present perfect.

EXERCISES

I. What is the use of future perfect? Give three examples.

Ans: (a)

(b)

(c)

II. Correct the following sentences.

(a) Will not have Manoj completed it by noon.

(b) I shall be complained it.

(c) Did he complained?

Ans: (a)

(b)

(c)

III. Use appropriate tense form of the verbs given in brackets.

(a) Rajendran (read) a novel yesterday.

(b) Rani (walk) in the street.

(c) Mr. Jain (read) a newspaper.

Ans: (a)

(b)

(c)

IV. Rewrite as directed.

(a) Was Leela doing her work. (Change into affirmative)

(b) They (play) football. (Write interrogative form of present simple)

(c) She came with me. (Change into present continuous)

Ans: (a)

(b)

(c)

24
Future Perfect Continuous (Form)

The form of future perfect continuous is as follows.

Shall have been/will have been + ing form of verb.

'Shall' is used with first person and will is used with second person and third person.

E.g. They will have been doing business for two years.
I shall have been working in a firm for the rest of my life.

Negative of future perfect is formed by adding 'not' after the auxiliary.

E.g. They will not have been doing business for two years.
I shall not have been working in a firm for the rest of my life.

Interrogative is formed by inverting auxiliary and subject.

E.g. Will they have been doing business for two years?
Shall I have been working in a firm for the rest of my life?

Negative interrogative is formed by putting 'not' after the subject in the interrogative sentence. Its contracted form is formed by adding 'n't' to the subject in interrogative sentence.

E.g. Will they not have been doing business for two years?
Shan't I have been working in a firm for the rest of my life?

EXERCISES

I. Write three examples for future perfect continuous.

Ans: (a)
(b)
(c)

II. Change the answers of exercise I into negative forms.

Ans: (a)
(b)
(c)

III. Change the answers of exercise I into interrogative form.

Ans: (a)
(b)
(c)

IV. Change the answers of exercise III into negative interrogative form.

Ans: (a)

(b)

(c)

25

Future Perfect Continuous (Use)

This tense form is used to express a future continuous activity which would start in the future.

E.g. Next year he will have been learning English for two years.

EXERCISES

I. Rewrite as directed.

(a) Birds are singing. (Change into negative)

(b) The earth revolves around the sun(Change into interrogative)

(c) They have seen me. (Change into negative interrogative contracted form)

(d) Next month they will have been working in the gold mine. (Change into Smple future)

Ans: (a)

(b)

(c)

(d)

II. Express the following ideas in sentences.

(a) Mr. Pradeep is an engineer. He started his work two years ago. He will continue his work.

(b) This year is 1999, Rajeev is selected for admission in the medical college. There he will study from 2000 to 2005.

Ans: (a)

(b)

III. What are the difference between future perfect continuous and past perfect continuous. Give two examples.

Ans:

GRAMMAR

CONTENTS

Sl. No.	Chapters	Exercise written date					Marks	Remarks
1.	Punctuation Marks							
2.	Comma							
3.	Semicolon and Colon							
4.	Interrogation mark – exclamation mark – inverted comma – apostrophe – quotation mark.							
5.	Negative formation							
6.	Interrogative formation							
7.	Reported Speech							
8.	Passive Voice							
9.	Mood							
10.	Concord							
11.	Model Auxiliaries							
12.	Conditionals							
13.	Preparatory 'there'/'it'							

1
Punctuation Marks

There are eight punctuation marks in English.
They are:
(1) Full stop (.)
(2) Comma (,)
(3) Interrogation mark (?)
(4) Exclamation mark (!)
(5) Colon (:)
(6) Semicolon (;)
(7) Inverted commas (‘ ’)
(8) Quotation marks (“ ”)
Let us see the uses of each punctuation marks.

FULL STOP

1. It is used at the end of a sentence other than interrogative and exclamation.

E.g. She is my sister.
Go and fetch your books.

2. It is used after abbreviations and initials.

E.g. M.A.
M.B.B.S
A. V. Mohan

EXERCISES

I. Name the following punctuation marks used.
(a) “Please come here.”
(b) Yes, I know that.
(c) 10:30
(d) Please put a ‘marks’ in the paper
(e) Who are you?

Ans: (a) (b)
(c) (d)
(e)

II. Please add necessary punctuation marks whenever required.
She said that she has passed B.Sc examination.

Ans:

III. Write punctuation marks.

(a) exclamation mark | (b) semicolon
(c) comma | (d) interrogation mark
(e) quotation marks

Ans: (a) (b)
(c) (d)
(e)

2
Comma

1. It is used after each noun in a sentence provided that (a) if the items are more than three in number (b) all the items have same verb.

E.g. Jayan, Raman, Krishnan and Sunil went to see a picture.

2. It is used to separate inserted clause in a sentence.

E.g. Mr. Shabu, the Manager, was suspended from the office.
She, my wife, is a beautiful woman.

3. It is used after each line of postal address (at the end of the last line full stop is used), and personal address.

E.g. Mr. Sathesh, H.No. 15A, Rajeev Gandhi Marg, Chennai.
Sir, you are my boss.

4. It is used to separate a subordinate clause in a sentence.

E.g. When I reached there, he left.
If you know me, tell my name.

EXERCISES

I. Rewrite the following sentences using punctuation marks wherever necessary.

(a) Reena Rani Rajani are my class mates.
(b) Please come Sir and help me.
(c) S N Book house M G Road Kochi
(d) J K Bose the managing director is going abroad.

Ans: (a)
(b)
(c)
(d)

II. Briefly describe the uses of 'comma'.

Ans:

3

Semicolon and Colon

SEMICOLON

1. Semicolon is used to separate closely related clauses in a sentence.

E.g. As fast as I travel, I get tired; as fast as I think, I get bored.

2. It separates clauses of a compound sentence having commas.

E.g. He is decent, innocent and broad minded; but he lacks courage.

COLON

1. It indicates the starting of a quotation.

E.g. Krishnan said: "I am your father".
He asked: "Who is coming here?"

2. It separates hour from minute, if it is mentioned in figures.

E.g. 10:30

E.g. 12:25

3. It is asked before the introduction of a list.

E.g. The things which I prefer are: tea, cigar and alcohol.

EXERCISES

I. Give three sentences in which semicolon is used.

(a)

(b)

(c)

II. What is the difference between a colon and a semicolon?

Ans:

III. Rewrite the following sentence using colon wherever necessary.

(a) Suma said "You are brave."
(b) 4 15 (four hours and fifteen minutes).
(c) My well wishers are Dileep, Pradeep and Dinesh.
(d) 3 05 (three hours and five minutes).

Ans: (a)

(b)

(c)

(d)

4

Interrogation Mark - Exclamation Mark - Inverted Comma - Apostrophe - Quotation Mark

INTERROGATION MARK

This punctuation mark is used at the end of an interrogative sentence.

E.g. What is your name?
Do you know me?

EXCLAMATION MARK

It is used at the end of an exclamatory sentence.

E.g. What a wonderful sight!
How beautiful it is!

INVERTED COMMA

Used to indicate a speciality of a word or words in a sentence.

E.g. The word 'the' is an article.
'Indian skeptic' is an English monthly.

APOSTROPHE

1. It is used to show omission of one or more letters.

E.g. don't, can't

2. It shows possessive case.

E.g. Ram's father, Sita's husband.

QUOTATION MARK

It shows direct speech.

E.g. Sita said "I am leaving".

EXCERCISE

I. Rewrite the following passage using punctuation marks wherever necessary.

Hearing this the other man told the thief that he too was as honest as his friend. In his words he had already sold out the land so it did not belong to him. Thus neither of them was willing to take it The chief then thought for a while and said one of you have a son and other has a daughter Let their marriage be done and give them the golden pot as a present.

Ans:

5
Negative Formation

Negative form of a sentence is made by putting the word 'not' after the auxiliary.

E.g. Who was reading?

↓

Who was not reading?

I am thinking.

↓

I am not thinking.

If the sentence do not carry an auxiliary split the verb as follows and put 'not' after the helping verb.

base form → do + base form (work = dc + work)

's' form → does + base form (works = does + work)

Past form → did + base form (worked = did + work)

E.g. She work in the field.

↓

She do not work in the field.

Some times 'never' is used instead of 'not' to make a sentence negative.

E.g. He can never read.

They will never come.

In spoken form contracted form of negative is used.

E.g. Please don't shout.

Won't you come?

Irregular contracted forms are:

won't = will not

shan't = shall not

Note: Care to omit the words 'always, often', etc from the affirmative sentence before adding 'not' to change it negative.

EXERCISES

I. Change the following sentences into negatives.

(a) She works.
(b) Who can read this?
(c) Did you finish the work?
(d) Suma wrote a letter.
(e) They have done it.

Ans: (a)
(b)
(c)
(d)
(e)

II. Change the following sentences into negatives by using 'never'.
(a) She reads novels.
(b) My mother always gives me money.

Ans: (a)
(b)

III. Change the followings into contracted forms.

(a) is not	(b) have not
(c) shall not	(d) would not
(e) were not	

Ans:

(a)	(b)
(c)	(d)
(e)	

6
Interrogative Form

There are three types of question forms in English.

(a) 'Yes' or 'no' questions.

(b) 'wh' questions.

(c) tag questions.

'Yes' or 'no' questions

Type of question is formed by inverting subject and auxiliary in sentences.

E.g. He has read a book.

↓

Has he read a book?

If the sentence do not carry an auxiliary verb, split the verb into helping verb (do, does or did) + base form as you have noticed in the chapter 'Negative Formation' and invert them as mentioned above.

E.g. She comes to school.

↓

Does she comes to school?

Negatives of this type of questions are formed by putting 'not' after the subject or 'n' t' after the auxiliary in the interrogative sentence.

E.g. Does she not come to school?

↓

Doesn't she come to school?

EXERCISES

I. Change the following sentences into 'yes' or 'no' questions.

(a) They know me very well.

(b) Mr. Rao is intelligent.

(c) Chandran and his wife explained the matter.

(d) He has been doing it.

(e) We shall tell the truth.

Ans: (a)

(b)

(c)
(d)
(e)

II. Change the answers of exercise I into negative form.

Ans: (a)
(b)
(c)
(d)
(e)

'Wh'-questions

This type of questions are formed by the following formula.

Question word + auxiliary + subject + verb + ...

E.g. What do you know?

Why do you go home?

If the positive sentence do not possess an auxiliary, split the verbs as follows and use it as in the word order given in the formula.

Dictionary form → do + base form.

's' form → does + base form.

Past form → did + base form.

E.g. Sheela goes home.

↓

Where does Sheela go?

Negative questions are formed by putting 'not' after the auxiliary verb. **E.g.** Why don't you go home?

What don't you know?

EXERCISES

I. Frame questions using the following question words.

(a) how long	(b) whom	(c) where
(d) what	(e) who	(f) how much
(g) why.		

Ans:

(a)	(b)	(c)
(d)	(e)	(f)
(g)		

II. Frame questions so that the underlined word(s) get(s) as answers.

(a) He can buy <u>a car</u>.

(b) <u>Mother</u> gives food to her children.

(c) He saw <u>a snake</u>.

Ans: (a)

(b)

(c)

TAG QUESTIONS

Tag questions or tail questions are formed by adding a question tag after putting a comma at the end of sentences.

The questions tag is formed by the following way.

auxiliary verb of the sentence + subject in pronoun + question mark.

Note: (1) If the first part carry 'not', the tail part should be positive.

(2) If the first part does not carry 'not' the tail part should carry 'not' in contracted form.

(3) If the first part does not carry an auxiliary verb, add auxiliary in the tail part as follows.

base form of verb - do

's' form of verb - does

past form of verb - did

(4) If the first part carries the auxiliary 'am', the tail part should contain the auxiliary 'are'.

E.g. He travelled long, didn't he?

Reena did not go home, did she?

I am handsome, aren't I?

EXERCISES

I. Supply proper question tag.

(a) She sings well, ...?

(b) Manu as well as his friends are absent...............?

(c) Sunil hardly knows the answer ....?

(d) He was so fat ....?

(e) I found I had scarcely any money ....?

(f) Many of us keep the love four our kins ....?

(g) I am not rich .... ?

(h) I can't buy a car ....?

(i) She gave birth to a child ....?

(j) The wind blows very hard ....?

Ans: (a)

(b)

(c)

(d)

(e)

(f)

(g)

(h)

(i)

(j)

II. Correct the followings.

(a) She is very rich, is she?

(b) Sudha and Suma dance, doesn't she?

Ans: (a)

(b)

7
Reported Speech

Reported form of a direct speech is called reported speech on indirect speech. Look at the following two sentences and note the difference.

Raju said: "I shall come tomorrow".

↓

Raju said that he would come tomorrow.

When you change a direct speech into indirect (reported) speech, the following changes should be made in the reported sentence.

(1) Quotation marks of the direct speech and the comma after the first clause is omitted.

(2) A connecting word is added between the two clauses. (In some rare cases this is waived).

(3) The pronouns 'I' and 'we' are changed to 'he' and 'they' respectively and 'me' and 'us' are changed to 'him' and them respectively.

(4) Auxiliaries are changed to their past forms as follows.

is/am → was
are → were
have/has → had
can → could
may → might
shall → should
will → would

EXERCISES

I. What is the difference between direct speech and indirect speech?

Ans:

II. What change should be made on the following words, when they are changed into indirect speech.

(a) many	(b) me	(c) are
(d) I	(e) us	(f) will

Ans:

(a)	(b)	(c)
(d)	(e)	(f)

III. What change should be made on the punctuation marks when the sentences that carry these marks are changed into indirect speech. Give one example.

Ans:

(5) Verbs are changed into their past forms.

(6) The following expressions are changed as given below.

this → that
these → those
thus → so
now → then
here → there
hither → thither
hence → thence
to-day → that day
tomorrow → the next day
yesterday → the previous day
last night → the previous night
ago → before

(7) Nominative of the address is brought to the first clause.

(8) In interrogative (wh- questions) sentences the connecting word should be asked/demanded/inquired.

(9) In 'yes' or 'no' questions the connecting word is 'asked + if/whether'.

EXERCISES

I. What changes should be brought to the following words, when the sentences that they carry change into reported speech.

(a) here	(b) yesterday	(c) these
(d) ago	(e) now	(f) tomorrow.

Ans:

(a)	(b)	(c)
(d)	(e)	(f)

II. Write true or false.

(a) 'I' in the direct speech changes into 'me' in reported speech.

(b) No change is needed in the verb when a sentence is changed from direct speech to indirect.

(c) The auxiliary 'may' remains unchanged in reported speech.

(d) The connecting words in exclamatory sentences (reported) one 'wondered + that'.

(e) Quotation marks of the direct speech remains unchanged in reported speech.

Ans: (a)
(b)
(c)
(d)
(e)

(10) In exclamatory sentences the connecting word should be exclaimed/ wondered + that. Exclamation words such as what/how etc. are omitted and 'great', 'big', 'very' etc. are added into the body of the reporting clause.

(11) In imperative sentences, the connecting word should be requested/ advised/ordered/asked/implored + to etc.

Note the examples given below

(1) Ramesh said "I am going to school".
Ramesh said that he was going to school.

(2) Ramesh "Who is going to school?"
↓
Ramesh asked who was going to school.

(3) Ramesh said "how beautiful it is!"
Ramesh exclaimed that it is very beautiful.

(4) Ramesh: "Do you know me?"
↓
Ramesh asked if I know him.

(5) Ramesh said, "Please bring me a glass of water".
↓
Ramesh requested to bring a glass of water.

(6) Ramesh said "I may come today".
↓
Ramesh said that he might come that day.

EXERCISES

I. Change the following sentences into indirect speech.
(a) "Hello", where are you going?"
(b) Rahim: "I want to reach the office early today."
(c) He said to the lady, "What are you going to drink?"
(d) "We can't have a big dog here", he said.
(e) "Have you been waiting here long", he asked to his friend.
(f) Radha said, "Please bring my books."
(g) He told me "Study well, otherwise you will fail."
(h) "What a wonderful sight", Krishnan said.

(i) She said, "I shall take it today".

(j) They said "We cannot come with you."

Ans: (a)

(b)

(c)

(d)

(e)

(f)

(g)

(h)

(i)

(j)

8
Passive Voice

There are two voices in English. They are active voice and passive voice.

If the subject of a sentence does the matter (i.e. active in nature), it is in the active voice.

E.g. Rama killed Ravana.

If the subject of a sentence does not do anything but merely allows something to be done to it, it is in the passive voice.

E.g. Ravana was killed by Rama.

Compare the above two examples. In the first example, the verb 'killed' is the action of 'Rama' who is the subject. Hence it is called in the active voice. But the second example is quite different. In it, the word 'Rama' merely allows the verb to be done to him.

When you change a sentence from active to passive, there are a few points to remember.

(a) The Subject of the active becomes the object of the passive and vice versa.

(b) The preposition 'by' is used before the object in the passive voice.

EXERCISES

I. Identify the voice of the following sentences.

(a) I need a change.
(b) He lived in India.
(c) A mango was eaten by him.
(d) The boy was not qualified.
(e) He passed by the post office.
(f) Ravana is being killed by Rama.
(g) He was passed in the examination.
(h) She was married by Vinod.
(i) Let the envelop be despatched.
(j) Who gave you this book?

Ans: (a)
(b)

(c)
(d)
(e)
(f)
(g)
(h)
(i)
(j)

(3) Verb Changes as follows.
Verb: work

	. Active	Passive
Present simple	works	is/am/are + worked
Present continuous	is/am/are + working	being + worked
Present perfect	has/have + worked	has/have + been + worked
Past continuous	was/were + worked	was/were + being + worked
Past Simple	worked	was/were +worked
Past perfect	had + worked	had + been + worked
Future simple	shall/will + work	shall/will + be + worked
Future continuous	shall/will + be + working	shall/will + be + being + worked
Future perfect	shall/will + have/has + worked	shall/will + has + have + been + worked.

Note: Present, past and future perfect continuous passive forms are uncommon.

EXERCISES

I. Change the following sentences into passive voice.
(a) I will kill you.
(b) She gave birth to a child.
(c) Nobody invited him.
(d) He saw a snake.
(e) He knows me well.
(f) we heard a shout.
(g) He is writing a novel.
(h) His teacher gave him a book.
(i) I saw a terrible dream.
(j) They were seeing a picture.

Ans: (a)
(b)

(c)

(d)

(e)

(f)

(g)

(h)

(i)

(j)

9
Mood

The three moods in English are: indicative, imperative and subjunctive.

INDICATIVE MOOD

Indicative mood of a verb always shows statement of fact and plain questions.

E.g. The cottage will be closed for a month.
What is its cost?

IMPERATIVE MOOD

Imperative mood of verb expresses advice, command and prayer.

E.g. You have to be tidy.
Don't drink.
Oh, God, give us pardon.

SUBJUNCTIVE MOOD

This mood expresses wish, desire, possibility, purpose and condition.

E.g. I wish I were a doctor.
God save us!
If I were rich, I would help you.
I am hoping that, it might rain tonight.

EXERCISES

I. Re-write as directed.
(a) I wish you were decent. (Change into imperative mood)
(b) I shall do it. (Change into imperative mood)

Ans: (a)
(b)

II. Find the mood of the following sentences.
(a) Let us move.
(b) May God help you!
(c) If I were you, I would have been married her.

(d) Who will come with me?
(e) Don't forget it.
(f) I shall help you.
(g) Will you do it?

Ans: (a)
(b)
(c)
(d)
(e)
(f)
(g)

10
Concord

There should be an agreement between the subject and verb in a sentence on number and person. It is called concord of the verb with the subject.

Look at the following sentences.

1. They works.
2. I are rich.

In the first sentence, the subject is third person plural. But the 's' form of the verb (work + s = works) is for the third person singular subject. Hence the sentence is wrong. It should be as follows.

They work.

In the second sentence subject is in first person singular. But the auxiliary is suitable only to first person plural, second person and third person plural. It can be corrected as follows.

I am rich.

Look at the table given below for the correct concord of 'be'.

Person	Singular	Plural
I	am, was	are, were
II	are, were	are, were
III	is, was	are, were

EXERCISES

I. Say whether the following sentences are correct or not.

(a) I has a car.

(b) Students was reading.

(c) I will go to my house.

Ans: (a)

(b)

(c)

II. Do as directed.

(a) Write the plural form of 'am'.

(b) Write singular form of 'were'.

(c) What is the third person singular forms of 'be'.

(d) What is the second person plural form of 'be'.

Ans: (a)

(b)

(c)

(d)

III. Correct the following sentences.

(a) We knows him.

(b) They was dancing in the hall.

Ans: (a)

(b)

Verb changes according to the subject is given in detail in the section 'tenses'. Carefully study the following points.

(1) Singular nouns connected by 'and' are normally followed by plural verb.

E.g. Ram and Rajan are going to school.

(2) If the subject contain more than one person or thing but considered as a whole, it is followed by singular verb.

Eg:- Five thousand rupees is a large amount.
His father and mother is kind.

(3) Expressions like 'neither ...... nor', 'either .... or' are followed by singular verbs, if they are connecting singular nouns and plural verbs, if they are connecting singular and plural or plural and plural nouns.

E.g. Neither Rajan nor Raju knows English.
Neither the teacher nor his students know English.

(4) Collective nouns are always followed by singular verbs.

E.g. The committee is considering your case.

(5) If the 'neither .... nor' or 'either … … or' are used to connect different persons, the verb follows the second noun.

E.g. Neither Suresh nor I have seen the film.

EXERCISES

I. Correct the following sentences.

(a) Leela and Suma is studying.

(b) Neither Suresh nor Mohan play football.

(c) Either he or I are thinking of it.

(d) One thousand rupees are lost in the game.

(e) Either his brother or his friends is brilliant.

Ans: (a)

(b)

(c)

(d)

(e)

II. What should be the verb if a collective noun comes as subject. Give two examples.

Ans:

III. Give one example each other than given, for the points given on last page.

Ans:

11
Modal Auxiliaries

The followings are the model auxiliaries in English: will, would, shall, should, can, could, may, might, must, ought to, need and dare.

Model auxiliaries are called so because they decide the mode or manner of the sentence.

They have common characteristics.

(a) They do not change according to the person and number of the subject.

(b) They never stand alone. They are used only to support a principal verb.

(c) They do not have infinitive or participle forms.

USES

WILL

The model auxiliary 'will' shows promise, determination, willingness and threat, if it is used with the first person ('I' and 'we').

E.g. I will kill him.
We will agree with you.
I will complete it.
It shows futurity if it is used with the second and third person.

E.g. He will pass the examination.

EXERCISES

I. What are the pecularities of model auxiliaries?

Ans:

II. What are the main model auxiliaries?

Ans:

III. Why model auxiliaries are called so?

Ans:

IV. Correct the followings.

(a) I to shall read it.

(b) They might it.

(c) She is caning it.

Ans: (a)

(b)

(c)

WOULD

It expresses willingness, wish, and preference.

E.g. I would like to know the truth.

He promised that he would help me.

I would rather die than marry her.

As it is the past form of 'will', it is used in the indirect speech in stead of 'will'.

E.g. The head master told that the school would closed for a week.

It is used to ask polite questions.

E.g. Would you give me your pen?

SHALL

The auxiliary 'shall' expresses promise, command, threat and determination, if it is used with the second and third person.

E.g. He shall sorry for this.

You shall get a reward.

The selection shall be according to merit.

It expresses simple futurity, if it is used with the first person.

E.g. I shall sign the document.

We shall meet again.

EXERCISES

I. Write three sentences having the model auxiliary 'would' that expresses 'wish'.

Ans:

II. Write three sentences having the model auxiliary 'will' that expresses threat.

Ans:

III. Correct the followings.

(a) I will rather write the examination than go to picture.

(b) You would get the money.

Ans: (a)

(b)

IV. What are the uses of 'will'?

Ans:

SHOULD

'Should' expresses obligation and distant possibility.

E.g. You should fight with him.

I should be able to read English.

It is used in the indirect speech instead of Shall.

E.g. He said that the thief should be hanged.

CAN

Can expresses permission and ability.

E.g. You can go home.

I can read English.

COULD

It shows past ability and possibility (on unreal condition).

E.g. I could drive motor car, when I was young.

You could pass, if you worked hard.

It is used to ask polite questions.

E.g. Could you come with me?

It is used in the indirect speech instead of 'can'.

E.g. Radha said that she could dance well.

EXERCISES

I. Write three sentences having the model auxiliary 'should' that expresses 'possibility'.

Ans: (a)

(b)

(c)

II. Write three sentences having the model auxiliary 'could' that expresses past ability.

Ans: (a)

(b)

(c)

III. Does the model auxiliary 'shall' give different meaning when used with first person and third person? Give two examples for each.

Ans:

MAY

'May' is used to expresses possibility, permission and wish.

E.g. It may rain tonight.
You may come with me.
May God bless you.

MIGHT

It is used to show, uncertain possibility.

E.g. Indian team might win the match.
It is used in the indirect speech instead of 'may'.

E.g. He said that he might pass the examination.

MUST

Must shows obligation, possibility, necessity and determination.

E.g. You must do it.
It must be reached you shortly.
I must do it, whether you wish or not.

OUGHT TO

It is used to show obligation, duty and necessity.

E.g. He ought to complete this.
I ought to advice him.
They ought to build a house.

EXERCISES

I. Write three sentences having the model auxiliary 'may' that expresses permission.

Ans:

II. Write three sentences having the model auxiliary 'must' that expresses determination.

Ans:

III. Write three sentences having the model auxiliary 'might' that expresses uncertain possibility.

Ans:

IV. What is the pecularity of the model auxiliary ought?

Ans:

NEED

Need is both an auxiliary and a verb. When it is used as an auxiliary, it is followed by 'not', 'hardly' or 'only'.

E.g. You need not do it.
I need hardly say that you are beautiful.
The past form of need is need + past participle of the verb.

E.g. They need not have thought of it.

DARE

'Dare' is like 'need'. It is also used as a principal verb and as an auxiliary.

As an auxiliary, it is commonly used with 'not' or it is used in interrogative sentences.

E.g. I dare not think of it.
How dare you are to question me?

EXERCISES

I. Write two sentences having model auxiliary 'dare'.

Ans:

II. What is the pecularity of the model auxiliary 'need'?

Ans:

III. Write the meaning of 'dare' when it is used as a principal verb. You may refer a dictionary.

Ans:

IV. Write two sentences having the word 'need' as principal verb.

Ans:

V. Write three interrogative sentences having the model auxiliary 'dare'.

Ans:

12
Conditionals

Clauses having the construction 'if' is always called conditional clauses.

There are three types of conditionals in English. They are:

(1) **First conditional**

If + present form of verb - will + infinitive

E.g. If she study hard, she will pass.

If he go home, he will see his father.

(2) **Second conditional**

If + past - would + infinitive

E.g. If she studied hard, she would pass.

If he went home, he would see his father.

(3) **Third conditional**

If + past perfect - would have + past participle.

Eg÷ If she had studied hard, she would have passed.

If she had gone home, he would have seen his father.

EXERCISES

I. What is a conditional clause? Give an example.

Ans:

II. Write three sentences as examples for the following sentence structure.

If + present form - will + infinitive.

Ans: (a)

(b)

(c)

III. Write three sentences as examples for the following sentence structure.

If + past perfect - would have + past participle.

Ans: (a)

(b)

(c)

IV. Complete the following sentences suitably.

(a) If I were a bird ....

(b) If he worked hard ....

Ans: (a)

(b)

13
Preparatory 'There' 'It'

Preparatory 'there'

Preparatory 'there' is used when we want to show something exists. The word order in such sentences is

there + verb + subject + ...

E.g. There is the book that you asked.

There exists one man in the hall.

Preparatory 'it'

The word order of the sentence containing preparatory 'it' is:

It + be + adjective/noun complement + ...

E.g. It is very nice of you.

It is my desire to pass the examination.

EXERCISES

I. Write five sentences with preparatory there:

Ans:

II. Write five sentences with preparatory 'it'.

Ans:

III. Rewrite as directed.

(a) Today is very cold. (begin the sentence with 'it')

(b) His father is there. (begin the sentence with 'that')

Ans: (a)

(b)

HOME STUDY SERIES - 5

COMPOSITION AND FORMS

P. V. GOPALAKRISHNAN

COMPOSITION

CONTENTS

Sl. No.	Chapter	Excerise Number	Page	Written date	Re-written date	Marks	Remarks
1.	Story Development						
2.	Letter Writing						
3.	Proverb Expansion						
4.	Short Essay						
5.	Comprehension						
6.	Precise Writing						

1
Story Development

Note

1. Read the outlines twice or thrice.
2. Classify the outlines into three or four groups according to the development of story.
3. Develop each group to paragraphs.
4. First paragraph is to introduce the story. In the first paragraph you have to give names to persons, animals and places.
5. Introduce dialogues.
6. Add a little humour to your story.
7. Give a suitable title to your story.

Example

Q. Develop the following hints into a readable story. Give your story a suitable title.

Anil and Suresh travelling by train .... Anil's ticket falls down .... Suresh picks it up .... Anil unawares of it .... ticket examiner coming .... Anil looks for ticket .... no ticket .... hides under seat .... Suresh gives ticket examiner two tickets .... "Where is the other man?".................. "Prefers to travel under the seat."

Ans:

The Man Who Travels Under the Seat

Anil and Suresh were neighbours. But they were not in good terms for a long period. However it was a misunderstanding that separated the two. Their family members considered themselves as members of one family even though they know that Anil and Suresh were not in good terms.

Once there was a competitive examination. Suresh and Anil were to go together in a train to the place where their examination centre is situated. They were met at the railway station. But both of them showed no sign of acquaintance. When the train steamed off both of them stepped into the same compartment.

After two hour's journey, the ticket examiner came. Anil, in order to take out the ticket, felt in his pocket. Alas .... there is no ticket! At the great confusion he thought of escaping from the punishment that reserved for the ticketless travellers. He was terrified by the thought. He thought of escaping by hiding. So he hid himself under a seat.

At the same time Suresh was stooping to pickup his handkerchief which was fallen. He found a ticket laying in the corridor between the two rows of the seats. He picked it up. He could learn that it was the ticket of Anil. He turned towards the direction of Anil but found the hidden Anil. Suresh learnt the matter. He never called Anil out. In the same moment the ticket examiner came near him and asked.

"Show your ticket please".

"Here, Sir", Suresh gave two tickets.

"Where is the other man?" Demanded the ticket examiner.

Suresh answered indicating Anil, "the other man prefers to travel under seat."

EXERCISES:

Q. 1. Develop the following hints into a readable story. Give a suitable title to your story.

Jester at King's Court .... cracks jokes .... king offended .... death sentence .... pleads for mercy .... freedom to choose manner of death .... "to die of old age" .... jester says.

Ans:

Q. 2. Develop the outline into a readable story and give a suitable title.

A Brahmin and his wife, Ganga .... a son .... the Brahmin keeps mongoose .... the Brahmin goes other village .... Ganga keeps little child in a cradle .... she tells mongoose to keep child .... mongoose sits near cradle .... a snake slowly creeps towards the cradle .... mongoose kills snake .... after some time Ganga comes back .... sees the mongoose with his face red with blood .... she cries .... throws pots on the mongoose .... the poor mongoose dies .... Ganga runs to cradle .... sees snake's dead body .... realises the thing .... cries.

Ans:

2

Letter Writing

Note

1. Write your address (don't include your name and date) at the right hand top corner of your letter, put commas after each line and a full stop at the end of the last line.
2. The salutation should be at the left hand side just below the date line. In personal letters salutation may be 'Dear Mr. Suresh', 'Dear Ms. Leela', 'My dear father' etc. In official letters salutation may be 'Dear Sir' or 'Respected Sir'.
3. The body of the letter should contain atleast three paragraphs. The first paragraph is to introduce the writer or the subject. Second paragraph is to message and the last paragraph is for conclusion.
4. Subscription, in the personal letters, may be 'Yours sincerely', 'Yours affectionately' and 'Yours lovingly'. In official letters subscription line is 'Yours faithfully'.
5. Put your signature under the subscription in official letters and name in personal letters.
6. In official letters the address of the recipient is to be placed at the left hand side under the date line and above the salutation. In personal letters it should be written in a box at the left hand corner under the signature.

Examples

Q. Write a letter to your uncle in Chennai requesting him to send you a book which you cannot get in your place.

An:s

22 C, Vikram Road
Kochi,
September 10, 1999.

My dear Uncle,

Received your letter which was sent on the occasion of my birthday. Thank you very much for the same. But you had never responded even though I had sent a replay. I was eager to hear from you.

While I am writing this letter, I have a very good intention of getting your favour once again, some of the English pronunciations confuse me very much. And so I would like to refer an English Pronuncing Dictionary for correct pronunciation. Such books are not available in our area. So please buy a copy of EPD from the sales division of Oxford University Press and send it to me at the earliest.

Our half yearly examination is in the next week. I don't like to bore you by putting more words in this letter. Extent my kind regards to everybody.

Hoping that you will send the book in the return post itself.

Yours affectionately
Ramesh

To,
Mr. Raveendran K. V.
Doctor's Colony,
T. Nagar
Chennai

Q. 2. You had sent a money order to your aunt fifteen days ago. But it has not reached her yet. Write a complaint to the Superintendent of Post Offices.

Ans:

22 C, Vikram Road,
Kochi,
September 10, 1999.

To
The Superintendent of Post Offices,
Kochi.

Sir,

This letter is to draw your attention into a very serious matter. I had sent a M.O. for Rs. 500/- (five hundred rupees) from the head Post Office, Kochi on 05-08-1999 (M.O. Receipt No: 136) to the following address. Radhika. R, Ram Vihar, P.O. Kozhikode - 21. About one month has passed since then. When I telephoned to my uncle, who is the husband of the addressee, it was revealed that the M.O. is not reached there.

I know not where it missed. She (the addressee) is in a very serious condition and in very much need of money. But I am also in a worst of condition. So that I am unable to send her another M.O.

So, please do an enquiry and take necessary action to get her money before she goes back to her maker.

Thanking you in anticipation.

Yours faithfully
Sd/-
Ramesh

Excercise

Q. 1. Write a letter to your father asking some money to celebrate your mid-summer vacation.

Ans:

Q. 2. Write a letter to the manager of a book stall ordering some books you need.

Ans:

3
Proverb Expansion

Note

1. Read the proverb three or four times and find what message it gives.
2. Define the proverb in one or two sentences.
3. Expand the message to four or five lines.
4. Add suitable examples.
5. Give relevent importance.

Examples

Q. 1. Expand the idea into a paragraph.

"All that glitters is not gold".

Ans:

A proverb is a short popular saying. It reveals some familiar truth. A wise saying always gives us some solid truth which has the power to save us from some danger. It gives some advice also. They are pearls among the golden treasure of moral stories. The proverb 'all that glitters is not gold' says that external appearance is misleading. We have seen decently dressed people. At the first sight we shall think that they are decent in their behaviour and character. But soon they themselves prove that they are like inwardly rotten beautiful fruits. So we should be aware of one fact that we cannot judge a thing seeing its external part only.

Q. 2. Expand the following idea into a paragraph.

"Birds of a feather flock together".

An:

A proverb is a short popular saying, long in use, embodying some familiar truth or useful thought in expressive and often picturesque language. This proverb depicts the human nature. Children play with children. Old men make company with old men. Drunkards prefer the company of drunkards. This is the truth that we see everywhere. So we should think of the company that we possess. If we are in bad company, but possess some good qualities, people won't consider it. They think of us as bad as the other members of our company. Thus the proverb says us to guard against external appearance.

Excercise

Q. 1. Develop the following idea into a paragraph.

"Health is wealth"

Ans:

Q. 2. Expand the idea into a paragraph.

"Rolling stone gathers no moss"

Ans:

4
Short Essay

Note

1. Introduce your idea.
2. Develop your idea adding examples, data and additional information.
3. Conclude your description.
4. Use simple sentences in your writing.
5. Avoid repetition.
6. Avoid unnecessary comments.

Examples

Q. 1. Write a short essay on a film that you have seen.

Ans:

A FILM I HAVE SEEN

I am not regular visitor in cinema theaters. I have seen only fifteen or sixteen films as yet. My father selects good pictures for me and give money to my elder brother. He would ask my brothers to take me also. The film that I remember most is the 'Jurassic Park'. It was a popular film. I couldn't understand most of the dialogues. However, it was interesting. The gene transfer and the development of Dinosaurs were enlightening. I could see the Dinosaurs who were once the rulers of the world.

I think the pictures that I have seen in science texts are nothing when compared to the huge size and terrific movements of the creatures of the film. In the next few nights my dreams were filled with Dinosaurs.

Q. 1. Write a short essay on your favourite book.

Ans:

MY FAVOURITE BOOK

I haven't read many books. The one that attracted me is the 'Adventures of Pinocchio'. It was written by Carlo Collodi. The story is simple and can be read with great interest. It tells the story of a marionette who wanted to become a real boy. At some stages, I identified the little Pinocchio with me. Pinocchio was always naughty. Disobedience was his motto.

Whatever his father told him, he did the opposite. Each time he was met with some difficulties. In my early years I was also such a boy. More or less I was disobedient. But when met with difficulties, I also changed like Pinocchio. This book contains a lot of good lessons. Each page is filled with advices. So growing children can find some profit with it. This one is interesting like the Panchathanthra.

Excercise

Q. 1. Write a short essay:

Need of Discipline

Or

An Accident You Have Seen.

Ans:

Q. 2. Write a short essay:

Your Hobby.

Or

A Journey You Have conducted.

Ans:

5
Comprehension

Note

1. Read the given passage at least three times.
2. Compare the questions with the sentences of the passage and find the relevant sentences.
3. Under line sentences which comply with the questions in idea.
4. Write answers in your own words.
5. Read your answers once again, correct mistakes and rewrite them if necessary.

Examples

Q. 1. Read the following passage and answer the questions given at the end.

"Reading maketh a full man". Bacon said. What great influence books exercise on men! Books can lead, guide and instruct men. At the same time, like bad company, they can also mislead man. I love books. They are my best friends. A book that I have read recently attracted me. It is a novel called *Christmas Carol* by Charles Dickens. The story is as follows.

Scrooge and Marley were business partners. Both of them were greedy and selfish. They had no friends at all. On one X'mas eve Marley died. Scrooge continued business alone. After seven years Marley's ghost appeared before Scrooge and promised to send three spirits to save Scrooge. One night three spirits appeared before Scrooge. They took Scrooge to several places and taught him what the meaning of X'mas was. The ghost of X'mas-yet-to Come showed him what his future would be.

These sight brought about a change in Scrooge's character. He decided to become a good man. He also decided keep up the spirit of Christmas all the year round and became a happy man. This novel conveying the message of goodness and charity to all.

1. Who were scrooge and Marley?

(a) friends (b) business men
(c) neighbours (d) business parterns.

2. What did the spirits teach scrooge?
(a) to earn more
(b) to love his business partner
(c) to make the business his own
(d) What the real meaning of X'mas was.

3. Book can lead man
(a) in the right path only
(b) in the wrong path only
(c) in the right path or wrong path according to the content
(d) in the way cf progress and prosperity.

4. Scrooge and Marley had no friends because
(a) they were cruel
(b) they were greedy and selfish
(c) they loved one another
(d) they hated every one

5. A book attracted me greatly. Here it means
(a) the book had an attractive look
(b) the book had attractive pictures
(c) the theme and story impressed me
(d) the price attracted me.

Ans:

1. (b) Business Partners.
2. (d) What the real meaning of X'mas was.
3. (c) In the right path or wrong path according to the content.
4. (b) They were greedy and selfish.
5. (c) The theme and story impressed me.

Q. 2. Read the following passage carefully and answer the questions given below.

One day Kaka Saheb found Gandhiji anxiously searching for something on his desk. "What is the matter? What are you looking for?" He asked. "I have lost my pencil." Bapu answered. "It was a very small pencil". Kaka Saheb was upset to see Babu wasting time and worrying about a little pencil. He took out his pencil and offered it to him. "No, no, I want my own little pencil." Bapu insisted. "Well use it for the time being" said Kaka Saheb. 'I'll find your pencie later. Don't waste time looking for it." "You don't understand that that little pencil is very precious to me." Babu insisted. "Natesan's little son gave it to me in Chennai. He gave it so much love and affection. I cannot bear to lost it."

Kaka Saheb didn't argue any more. He joined Gandhiji in the search.

At last they found it, a tiny piece, hardly two inches long. But Gandhiji was delighted to get it back. To him it was no ordinary pencil. It was the token of a child's love and to Bapu a child's love was very precious.

1. What was Gandhiji anxiously searching for?
2. Why Kaka Saheb was upset?
3. What did Kaka Saheb offer to Gandhiji?
4. Who gave the pencil to Gandhiji?
5. "At last they found it." What did they find?
6. "To Gandhiji it is no ordinary pencil." Then what was it to him?
7. How did Bapu consider the love of a child?

Ans:

1. Gandhiji was anxiously searching for a little pencil.
2. Kaka Saheb was upset to see Bapu wasting time and worrying about a little pencil.
3. Kaka Saheb offered Gandhiji his own pencil.
4. Natesan's little son gave the pencil to Gandhiji.
5. They found a little pencil hardly two inches long.
6. It was the token of a little child, a very precious thing for Gandhiji.
7. Bapu considered the love of a child a very precious thing.

EXERCISES

Q. 1. Read the following passage carefully and answer the questions given below.

Chris and his sister Curly went to Mumabi for a holiday with their mother. The children had always wanted to see the beach. The mother had saved some money. At last their long-awaited dream was fulfilled.

One morning as the two children were playing on the beach they saw a wounded crab struggling to reach the water. They had been told that crabs brought good luck. They carried the crab home and asked their mother if they could keep him as a pet. The mother said "we will be going back to Poona after two days and you'll both go to school. Go put it back in the sea".

The children did not like the idea of going back so soon. They decided to put it back in the water.

They found a safe looking corner near the shore, where the current was low and gently put the crab there. Then they saw a shining object lying under the water. It was a beautiful diamond ring. They picked it and ran home.

Then the three went to the police station to report the matter. The inspector said "This ring belongs to a very rich cloth merchant's wife. There is a big reward for it. You'll get it because, you have found the ring".

1. At last their long-awaited dream was fulfilled". What was their dream?
2. What did the children see, while they were playing?
3. Where they will be going after two days?
4. What was the shining object?
5. Where did they go with the ring?
6. Whose ring was it?
7. Was the crab lucky? Give a reason for your answer.

Ans:

1.
2.
3.
4.
5.
6.
7.

Q. 2. A gentlemen once advertised for a boy to assist him in his office and nearly fifty boys applied for the job. After a short time he chose one out of the whole number and sent all the rest away. "I should like to know" said a friend", "on what grounds you chose that boy". He had not a single recommendation with him. "you are mistaken" answered the gentle man. He had a great many. He wiped his feet when he came in, and close the door after him showing that he was orderly and tidy. He gave up his seat instantly to that lame old man, showing that he was courteous. He lifted up the book which I had purposely placed on the floor, and put it on the table, while all the rest stepped over it or push it aside. When I talked with him, I noticed that his clothes were carefully brushed, his hair in nice order, and his teeth as white as milk. When he wrote, he waited quietly for his turn instead of pushing the others aside. Don't you call these letters of recommendations? I do, and when I can tell you about a boy using my eyes for ten minutes, is worth all the five letters he can bring me".

Choose the most suitable alternative to complete each of the following sentences:-

1. The gentleman intrerviewed for the job

   (a) Only one boy (b) A few boys

   (c) Fifty boys (d) About fifty boys

2. The gentlemen's friend said that
   (a) The boy was very good choice
   (b) The boy was not qualified
   (c) The boy was without a recommendation
   (d) The interview was not properly conducted
3. The gentleman told his friend that
   (a) He was right
   (b) The boy had a recommendation
   (c) The boy had no recommendation
   (d) The boy had no formal recommendation
4. The gentleman found that the boy was orderly and tidy because
   (a) He had washed himself and put on clean clothes.
   (b) He wiped his feet when he came in and closed the door after him.
   (c) He had combed his hair and brushed his teeth.
   (d) He was soft spoken and gentle in manners.
5. The boy showed his politeness
   (a) By greeting the gentleman
   (b) By refusing to take the seat offered by the gentleman
   (c) By lifting up the book which had been placed on the floor
   (d) By giving up his seat instantly to a lame old man
6. The gentleman asked the question "don't you call these letters of recommendations" to
   (a) His friend (b) The lame man
   (c) The boy (d) The readers
7. The gentleman says that he can judge the qualities of the boy
   (a) Only with letters of recommendations
   (b) Even without using his eyes
   (c) By observing him for ten minutes
   (d) By listening to what others say about him

Ans: 1.

2.

3.

4.

5.

6.

7.

6
Precis Writing

Note

1. Read the passage until you get an idea of the contents.
2. Find the important points avoiding repeated sentences and examples.
3. Rewrite the important points in your own words.
4. Care to write the precis as the writing of a third person.
5. The length of the precis have to be one-third of the passage.
6. Read the rough summary (precis) that you have just prepared and do necessary corrections.
7. Rewrite the corrected rough summary.
8. Supply a suitable title.

Example

Q. Reduce the passage given below to one-third of its length.

Sai Baba and The National Integration Committee believes that the singing of Sai Bhajans would lead to national integration. Several hours of the T.V. channels are used for this purpose. It would create only another cult and would start fighting other cults.

If the Hindu, Muslim and Christian blood is donated to each other, the person who gets the blood will not fight the person who donated the blood and his religion. We can bring national integration in this way only. Everywhere we have our members they have started Blood Banks. We have to do this service everywhere we have members and groups.

Likewise we would be publishing in 'Indian Skeptic' other acts by which we can take action against the frauds.

(INDIAN SKEPTIC)

Ans:

New Mode for National Integration (Rough)

Singing of Sai Bhajans would create only fight among cults. Inter-religious blood donation is the best method for national integration. They have blood banks wherever they have members. 'Indian Skeptic' would publish further actions against frauds.

New Mode for National Integration

Singing of Sai Bhajans would create only fight among cults. Inter-religious blood donation is the best method for national integration. They have blood banks wherever they have members. 'Indian Skeptic' would publish further actions against frauds.

EXCERCISE

Q. 1. Reduce the passage given below to one-third of its length.

Criminal reformation is easier said than done. Criminal reformation is intricately interconnected with various facets of social life and the body polity. It is not enough if the change comes in the criminals. It requires corresponding changes in the outlook of the people, administration, criminal justice system and law enforcing authorities. In effect, criminal reformation is interwined with building alternate way of life–both for the criminals and their dependants. It is much more so when crime becomes their profession and they are dubbed as the criminal tribe and segregated into the settlements depriving them from normal interaction with the rest of the society for generation.

(ATHEIST)

Ans:

Q. 2. Prepare a summary of the passage given below reducing it one third of its length.

Ans:

Caste distinction is but man made. There is no reason whatsoever to think of it as God-ordained. We see from Nature that a lizard is not like a leach, nor a squirrel like a lizard, nor the poisonous lizard like a squirrel; no sheep is like a poisonous lizard, nor elephant is like a sheep; neither horse is like an elephant nor man is like a horse. Further, paddy is not like grass, the teak tree is not like the coconut tree. Neither water is like earth, nor fire like water, neither air is like fire nor the sky like air. Thus we see that all objects, movable and immovable in this universe, have been created with particular differentiating forms and natures that could be easily distinguished even by boys. Can that power, which can thus create, be in capable of creating the necessary marks of distinction in men too, to show that he has ordained several castes in the human race as, Brahman, Kshatriya, Vaisya and Shudra? Alas! a great pity!

(SIVAYOGI)

Ans:

FORMS

CONTENTS

Sl. No.	Chapter	Excerise Number	Page	Written date	Re-writen date	Marks	Remarks
1.	Application for Job	1					
		2					
2.	Form for membership	1					
		2					
3.	Bio-data Form	1					
		2					
4.	Pay-in-slip of Bank	1					
		2					
5.	Draft Form	1					
		2					
6.	Telegraph Form	1					
		2					
7.	Acknowledgement	1					
		2					
8.	Money Order Form	1					
		2					
9.	Postal Order	1					
		2					

1
Application for Job

Given below is a typical application form. Read the details before filling up an application form. An example is given on overleaf.

FORM OF APPLICATION

APPLICATION FOR THE POST OF ....

1. Name (IN BLOCK LETTERS) :
2. Father's Name/Husband's Name :
3. Date of Birth :
4. Employment Exchange Registration No. with Name of Employment Exchange :
5. Educational Qualifications :
6. Experience if any with details :
7. Whether belong to SC/ST/OBC :
8. Permanent Address :
9. Present Address for correspondence :
10. Extra curricular activities. If any. :
11. Remarks :

I do hereby declare that the particulars as mentioned vide. Sl. No. 1 to 9 above are correct.

Place:
Date:

(*Signature of the Applicant*)

Example

Q. Imagine that you are Mr. Sanjeevan M. N., C-25, T. Nagar, Mumbai - 400 027. Your date of birth is 25-4-73 and qualification is M.A. and type writing. Also imagine that your father's name is Madhavan Nair. Prepare an application for the post of clerk in the prescribed form.

(1) (11) (10) (9)

INDO-TIBETAN BORDER POLICE RECRUITMENT REGISTRATION FORM

NAME OF POST APPLIED FOR: Clerk

PLACE: Mumabi DATE: 24-9-99

1. Name: Sanjeevan M. N
2. Father's Name: Madhavan Nair
3. Permanent Home Address: C-25, T. Nagar, Mumbai
   Post Office: 400027 Police Station: T. Nagar
   District: Mumbai State: Maharashtra
4. Present Adress: C-25, T. Nagar, Mumbai
   Post Office: 400027 Police Station: T. Nagar
   District: Mumbai State: Maharashtra
5. Education: M. A., Type Writing
6. Date of Birth: 25-4-73
7. OUT OF FOLLOWING WITH WHICH CATEGORY YOU BELONG TO:
   GENERAL ✓, SCHEDULED CASTE, SCHEDULED TRIBE, O.B.C., EX-SERVICE

Space for PHOTOGRAPH (12)

Above given information is correct to the best of my knowledge and belief. I will be liable to be rejected in case of information given above found to be false or incomplete.
I have never been medically rejected earlier by ITBP recruitment board.

Sanjeevan (8)
Signature of Candidate

Notes:

1. Write your name as seen in certificates.
2. Write father's name in full.
3. Write complete postal address (permanant).
4. Write your address for present correspondence.
5. Write your qualification.
6. Write date of birth as seen in certificates.
7. Put a tick mark at the above item which is applicable.
8. Put your signature.
9. Write the date of filling up of the application.
10. Write name of post applied for.
11. Write the name of place from which you are sending the application.
12. Affix a recent passport size photograph of yours.

EXERCISE

1. Imagine that you are Mr. Mahesh. And your particulars are as shown

below. Fill up the given proforma.
Father's name: Babu, Date of Birth: 25-5-1975, Qualifications: Diploma in fire fighting, BSc, Category: SC, Experience: Nil.

PROFORMA

Application for the post of Fireman Gr. II

1. Name (In full/block letter) :
2. Father's Name :
3. Date of Birth :
4. Full address for communication :
5. Qualification :
6. Whether General (Unreserved)/OBC/SC/ST
7. Authentic documents as proof of adequate knowledge of operational use of fire fighting equipments :
8. Experience, if any

Recent Passport size Photo of the applicant

(Signature of Applicant)

2. Fill up the following application form. Write down your own particulars.

FORMAT FOR APPLICATION FOR THE POST OF SI (STENO) (Gr. - III) IN CRPF.

1. Full Name (in block letters)..
2. Father's Name & Occupation : ....
3. Name of Centre to appear in examination : ....
4. Permanent home address : ....
5. Present postal address : ....
6. Nationality : ....
7. Sex (Male/Female) : ....
8. Date of Birth (in Christian era) :..................
9. Whether SC/ST/OBC/General : ....
10. Education Qualification : ....
11. Indicate Medium (English or Hindi) for written test, Type Writing test and Shorthand test : ....
12. Particulars of extra curricular activities, if any ....
13. Have you been member of NCC ? ....
14. Are you married ? If so, state whether you have more than one spouse living ....
15. Particulars of present employment, if any ....
16. List of enclosures (No. & date of Crossed Indian Postal Order) : ....
17. Post applied for :..

Paste recent passport size photograph.

DECLARATION :- I hereby declare that all statements made in this application are true, complete and correct to the best of my knowledge and belief. In the event of any information being found false or incorrect or ineligibility being detected before or after test/interview, my candidature will stand cancelled and all my claim for recruitment forfeited. I also understand that if at any state I am found to have used unfair means in the written examination/test or to have violated any of the rule/regulation governing the conduct of the selection process, my candidature can be cancelled or be declared to have been failed by the selection board at its sole discretion.

Full signature of Candidate.

2
Form for Membership

A typical membership form should show all the personal data of a man. Look below for a typical membership form.

K. R. MEMORIAL PUBLIC LIBRARY
Application for Membership

1. Name in full (in capitals) :
2. Sex (male/female) :
3. Age (in completed years) :
4. Postal address (give pin code) :
5. Occupation :
6. Educational Qualification :
7. Name, position and address of a local person who knows the applicant well :
8. Declaration: I have read the rules and regulations of the Library and promise to abide by them.

Place:
Date:

Signature of applicant

K. R. MEMORIAL PUBLIC LIBRARY

Application for membership

1. Name in full (in capitals : *MOHAN. P.*
2. Sex (male/female) : *Male*
3. Age (in completed years) : *35 years*
4. Postal address (give pin code) : *RamVihar, T. Nagar Chennai: - 17*
5. Occupation : *Teaching*
6. Educational Qualification : *B. A. (English)*
7. Name, position and address of a local person who knows the applicant well : *K. Venu, Manager, Co-operativeUbran Bank, Chennai - 17*
8. Declaration : I have read the rules and regulations of the Library and promise to abide by them.

(9) Place : *Chennai*

(10) Date : *25-10-99*

Mohan 25/10/99
Signature of applicant (11)

Note:

1. Write your name in capital letters.
2. State whether the applicant is male or female.
3. Show your age.
4. Write your present postal address.
5. State what you are doing.
6. Write your educational qualification(s).
7. Write the name and postal address of a local person who has a little responsibility over you.
8. Write a declaration.
9. Write the name of place where you are staying.
10. Mention the date on which you signed the paper.
11. Put your signature.

EXERCISE

Q. 1. Fill up the application form given below.

K. R. MEMORIAL PUBLIC LIBRARY
Application for Membership

1. Name in full (in capitals) :
2. Sex (male/female) :
3. Age (in completed years) :
4. Postal address (give pin code) :

5. Occupation :
6. Educational Qualifications :

7. Name, position and address of a local person who knows the applicant well. :
8. Declaration: I have read the rules and regulations of the Library and promise to abide by them.

Place:
Date: **Signature of applicant**

Q. 2. Fill up the application form given below for your friend.

K. R. MEMORIAL PUBLIC LIBRARY
Application for Membership

1. Name in full (in capitals) :
2. Sex (male/female) :
3. Age (in completed years) :
4. Postal address (give pin code) :

5. Occupation :

6. Educational Qualification :

7. Name, position and address of a local person who knows the applicant well :
8. Declaration: I have read the rules and regulations of the Library and promise to abide by them.

Place:
Date:

Signature of applicant

3
Bio Data Form

A bio-data is used for sending alongwith an application for employment especially in private sector. There is no fixed form for it. But it should show important personal data.

BIO DATA

Name	:
Address	:
Age	:
Sex	:
Educational Qualification	:
Other Qualifications	:
Experience	:
Language Known	
read	:
write	:
speak	:
Expected salary	:

BIO DATA

1.	Name	: RAMESH. C
2.	Address	: TC 35/A, KOLKATA- 16.
3.	Age	: 27 Years
4.	Sex	: MALE
5.	Educational Qualifications	: B.Sc. (Physics) Computer Diploma
6.	Other Qualifications	: NIL
7.	Experience	: NIL
8.	Languages Known	
	read	: ENGLISH, HINDI, BENGALI
	write	: " " "
	speak	: " " "
9.	Expected salary	: Rs. 5000/- p.m

9. Expected Salary : 3000 p.m.

Note:

1. Write your name.
2. Write your postal address.
3. Mention your age.
4. Mention your sex.
5. State your educational qualification.
6. Mention other qualifications such as driving licence, certificate in sports etc.
7. Mention experience.
8. Mention languages that you know.
9. Mention expected salary.

EXERCISE

Q. 1. Prepare a bio-data.

Ans:

Q. 2. Prepare a bio-data.

Ans.

Q. 1. Prepare a bio-data for your friend.

Ans:

4

Pay-In-Slip of Bank

Most of the Banks have such type of forms. Hence learning of one will enable a man to fill up any such form. One example is given on overleaf.

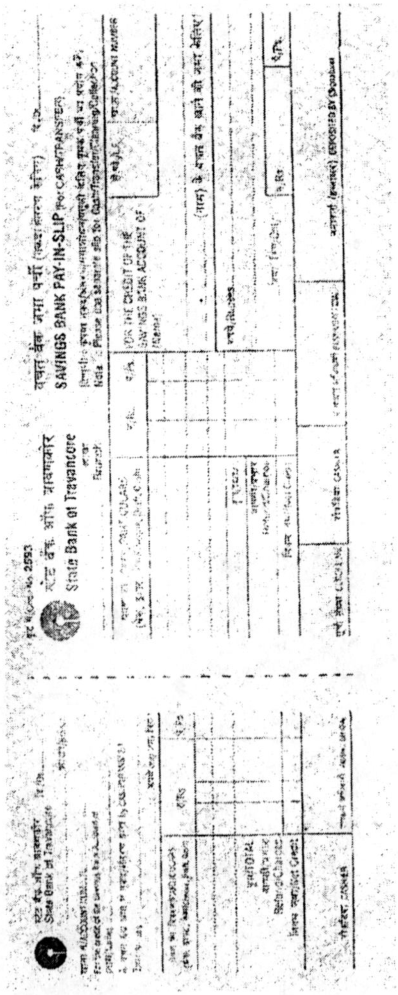
State Bank of Travancore
SAVINGS BANK PAY-IN-SLIP (For CASH/TRANSFER)
FOR THE CREDIT OF THE SAVINGS BANK ACCOUNT OF

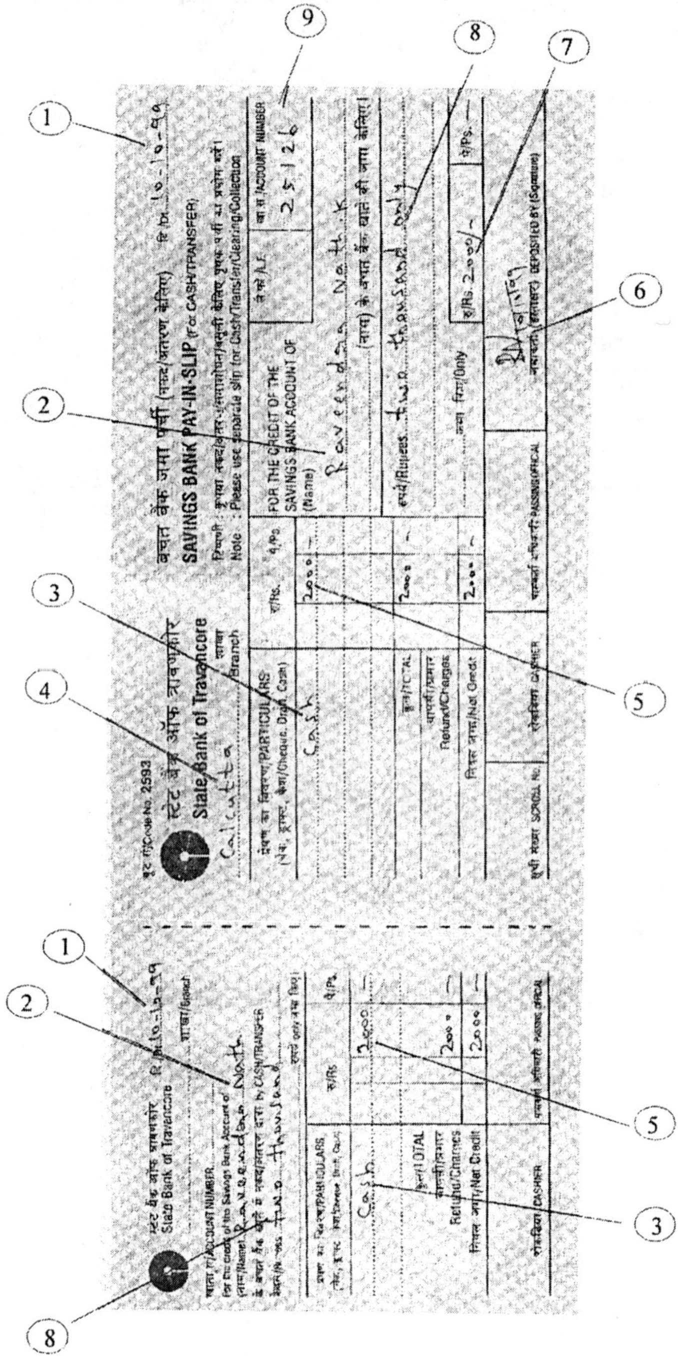
State Bank of Travancore
SAVINGS BANK PAY-IN-SLIP (For CASH/TRANSFER)
Note : Please use separate slip for Cash/Transfer/Clearing/Collection
FOR THE CREDIT OF THE SAVINGS BANK ACCOUNT OF (Name)
ACCOUNT NUMBER
PARTICULARS
TOTAL
Refund/Charges
Net Credit
CASHIER
DEPOSITED BY (Signature)
Calcutta
Cash
2000
Raveendran Nath. K
25126
two thousand only

Note:

1. Write the date of filling up the application form.
2. Write your name.
3. State in which mode you are paying the amount.
4. Write the name of bank branch in which you are depositing.
5. Write in figures the amount that you are depositing.
6. Put your signature.
7. Write in figures the amount that you are depositing.
8. Write in letters, the amount that you are depositing.
9. Write the account number as shown in your bank passbook.

EXERCISE

Q. 1. Deposit Rs. 5000. Your name is Chopra and account number is 25127.

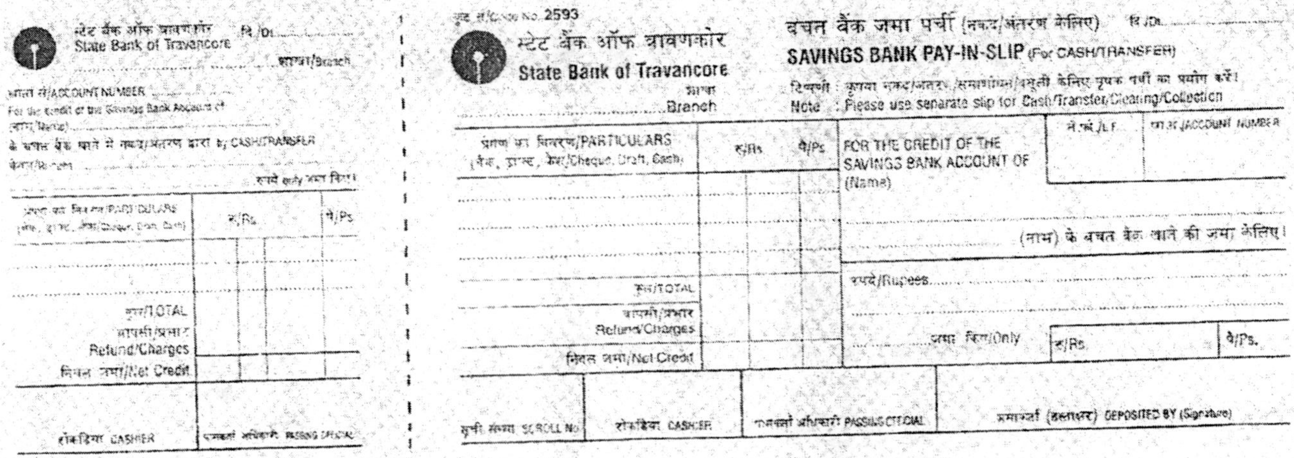

EXERCISE

Q. 2. Deposit Rs. 525. Your name is Kiran and account number is 15132.

स्टेट बैंक ऑफ त्रावणकोर
State Bank of Travancore

खाता सं ACCOUNT NUMBER

For the credit of the Savings Bank Account of

कुल/TOTAL

वापसी/प्रभार Refund/Charges

निवल जमा/Net Credit

रोकड़िया CASHIER

क्रम सं/Serial No 2593

स्टेट बैंक ऑफ त्रावणकोर
State Bank of Travancore

शाखा .... Branch

बचत बैंक जमा पर्ची (नकद/अंतरण केलिए)
SAVINGS BANK PAY-IN-SLIP (For CASH/TRANSFER)

Note : Please use separate slip for Cash/Transfer/Clearing/Collection

विवरण/PARTICULARS (चैक, ड्राफ्ट, नकद/Cheque, Draft, Cash)	रु/Rs	पै/Ps
कुल/TOTAL		
वापसी/प्रभार Refund/Charges		
निवल जमा/Net Credit		

FOR THE CREDIT OF THE SAVINGS BANK ACCOUNT OF (Name) ....

ले.फो./L.F.	खाता सं/ACCOUNT NUMBER

(नाम) के बचत बैंक खाते को जमा कीजिए।

रुपये/Rupees .... मात्र/Only

रु/Rs.	पै/Ps.

सूची संख्या SCROLL No	रोकड़िया CASHIER	पासकर्ता अधिकारी PASSING OFFICIAL	जमाकर्ता (हस्ताक्षर) DEPOSITED BY (Signature)

5

Draft Form

A draft is used to send money from one place to another place through a bank. The following form is used for that. The following page shows how it is filled.

STATE BANK OF TRAVANCORE

..............................Br./Date..............

For Shri/Smt...............................

..............................On account of

D.D./M.T.on..............................Br.

Favouring..............................

	Rs			P
Amount				
Exchange				
P&T Charges				
TOTAL				

Cash/Trf. Scroll No..............................

Cashier/Teller..............................

Passing Official..............................

Denomination/ No.of pieces		Rs.		P.
500x				
100x				
50x				
20x				
10x				
5x				
2x				
1x				
Coins				
TOTAL				

Cash/Trf. Scroll No..............................

Cashier/Teller..............................

Entd. by..............................

Passing official..............................

STATE BANK OF TRAVANCORE
DRAFT/MAIL TRANSFER REQUISITION

..............................Branch Date..............................

Please issue a D.D./M.T. on..............................Branch

For Rupees..............................

..............................only in favour of

				Rs. P.
Amount				
Exchange				
P&T Charges				
TOTAL				

Asst. Mgr. (Acts)/Mgr. .... Signature of the Applicant

D.D./M.T. No.............................. Name & Address

Received the draft

Signature

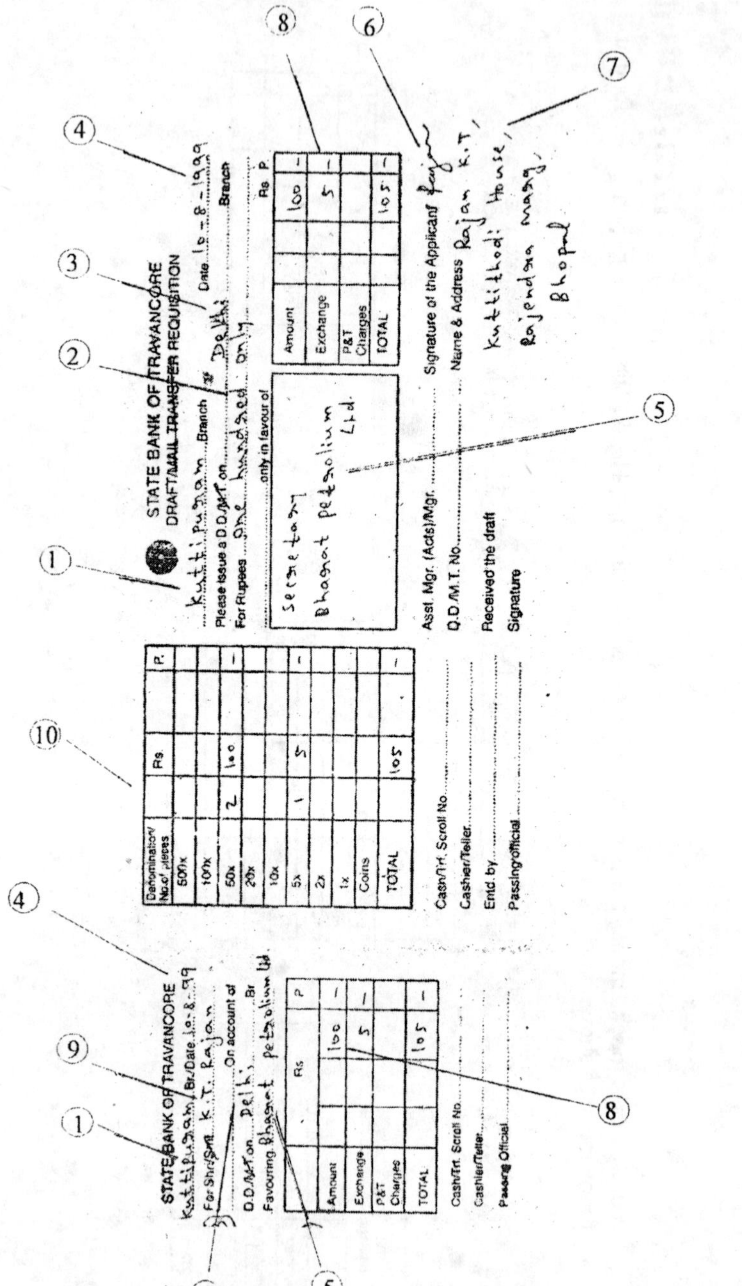
STATE BANK OF TRAVANCORE
Kuttipuram Br/Date 10-8-99
For Shri/Smt. K.T. Rajan
On account of
D.D./M.T. on Delhi Br
Favouring Bhagat petrolium Ltd
Rs P
Amount 100 -
Exchange 5 -
P&T Charges
TOTAL 105 -
Cash/Trf. Scroll No.
Cashier/Teller
Passing Official
Denomination/No. of pieces Rs. P.
500x
100x
50x 2 100 -
20x
10x
5x 1 5 -
2x
1x
Coins
TOTAL 105 -
Cash/Trf. Scroll No.
Cashier/Teller
Entd. by
Passing official
STATE BANK OF TRAVANCORE
DRAFT/MAIL TRANSFER REQUISITION
Kuttipuram Branch Date 10-8-1999
Please issue a D.D./M.T. on Delhi Branch
For Rupees One hundred only
only in favour of
Secretary Bhagat petrolium Ltd.
Rs P
Amount 100 -
Exchange 5 -
P&T Charges
TOTAL 105 -
Asst. Mgr. (Accts)/Mgr.
Signature of the Applicant Rajan
D.D./M.T. No.
Name & Address Rajan K.T., Kuttithodi House, Rajendra marg, Bhopal
Received the draft
Signature
1
2
3
4
5
6
7
8
9
10

Note :

1. Write the name of bank branch from which the draft is going to take.
2. Write the amount in letters.
3. Write the name of bank branch from which the draft is going to encash.
4. Write the date on which you wish to take the draft.
5. Write the name of person or institution for whom the amount is to be sent.
6. Put your signature.
7. Write your name and address.
8. Write the amount of DD, bank charge, and total amount.
9. Write your name.
10. Show in which denomination of cash you give at the bank counter alongwith the DD form.

EXERCISE

Q. 1. Fill up the following draft form in favour of Prakash Book Depot, Bareilly. The amount that you are sending is Rs. 200 (two one hundred notes). Bank charge for that is Rs. 10/-.

STATE BANK OF TRAVANCORE

........................Br./Date..................

For Shri/Smt..

....On account of

D.D./M.T.on.......................................Br.

Favouring..

	Rs			P
Amount				
Exchange				
P&T Charges				
TOTAL				

Cash/Trf. Scroll No.......................................

Cashier/Teller..

Passing Official..

Denomination/ No.of pieces		Rs.		P.
500x				
100x				
50x				
20x				
10x				
5x				
2x				
1x				
Coins				
TOTAL				

Cash/Trf. Scroll No.......................................

Cashier/Teller..

Entd. by...

Passing official..

STATE BANK OF TRAVANCORE
DRAFT/MAIL TRANSFER REQUISITION

....Branch Date..............................

Please issue a D.D./M.T. on...Branch

For Rupees ....

....only in favour of Rs. P.

Amount				
Exchange				
P&T Charges				
TOTAL				

Asst. Mgr. (Acts)/Mgr. .... Signature of the Applicant

D.D./M.T. No.. Name & Address

Received the draft

Signature

EXERCISE

Q. 2. Fill up the following draft requisition form in favour of National Oil Company, New Delhi. The amount of draft is Rs. 5000/-. Bank charges for that is Rs. 50/-. You are giving 10 five hundred notes.

STATE BANK OF TRAVANCORE

..................................Br./Date..................

For Shri/Smt. ....

......................................On account of

D.D./M.T.on. ....Br.

Favouring..

	Rs			P
Amount				
Exchange				
P&T Charges				
TOTAL				

Cash/Trf. Scroll No. ....

Cashier/Teller..

Passing Official.......................................

Denomination/ No.of pieces		Rs.		P.
500x				
100x				
50x				
20x				
10x				
5x				
2x				
1x				
Coins				
TOTAL				

Cash/Trf. Scroll No. ....

Cashier/Teller..

Entd. by...

Passing official.......................................

STATE BANK OF TRAVANCORE
DRAFT/MAIL TRANSFER REQUISITION

..................................Branch   Date..................

Please issue a D.D./M.T. on ....Branch

For Rupees ....

..................................only in favour of   Rs. P.

Amount				
Exchange				
P&T Charges				
TOTAL				

Asst. Mgr. (Acts)/Mgr. ....   Signature of the Applicant

D.D./M.T. No. ....   Name & Address

Received the draft

Signature

6
Telegram Form

Telegram is used for extending urgent message. The following form is used for that. Fill it up and give it to the telegram booking clerk in the post office.

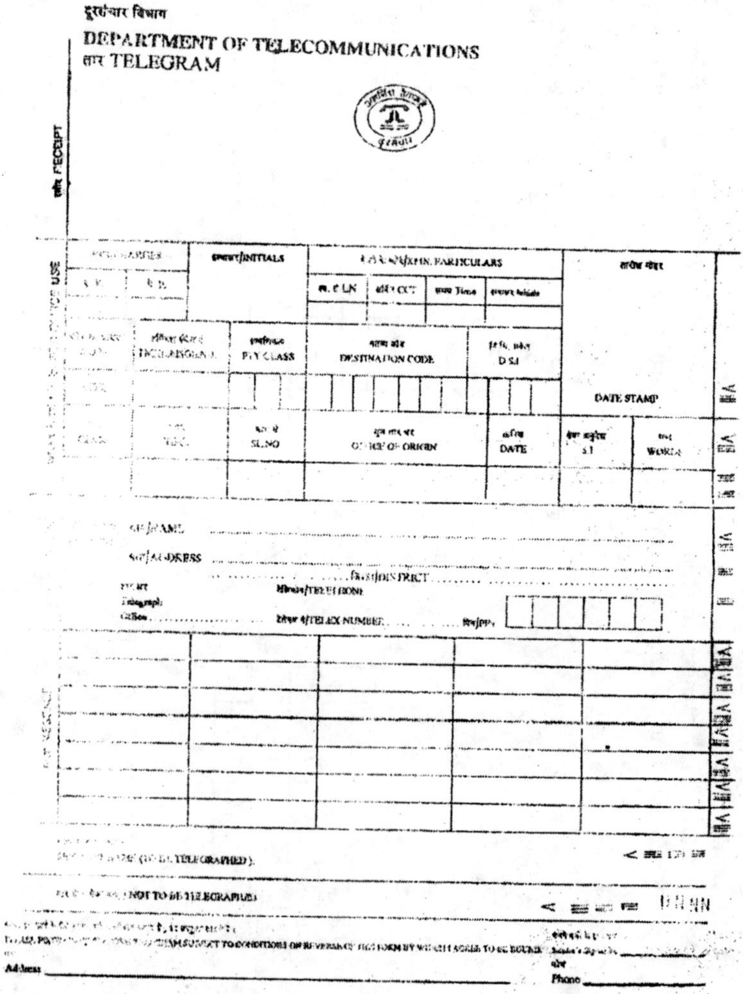
दूरसंचार विभाग
DEPARTMENT OF TELECOMMUNICATIONS
तार TELEGRAM
INITIALS
PARTICULARS
Time
DATE STAMP
P.Y. CLASS
DESTINATION CODE
D.S.I
SL.NO
OFFICE OF ORIGIN
DATE
WORDS
NAME
ADDRESS
DISTRICT
TELEPHONE
TELEX NUMBER
(TO BE TELEGRAPHED)
(NOT TO BE TELEGRAPHED)
Address
Phone

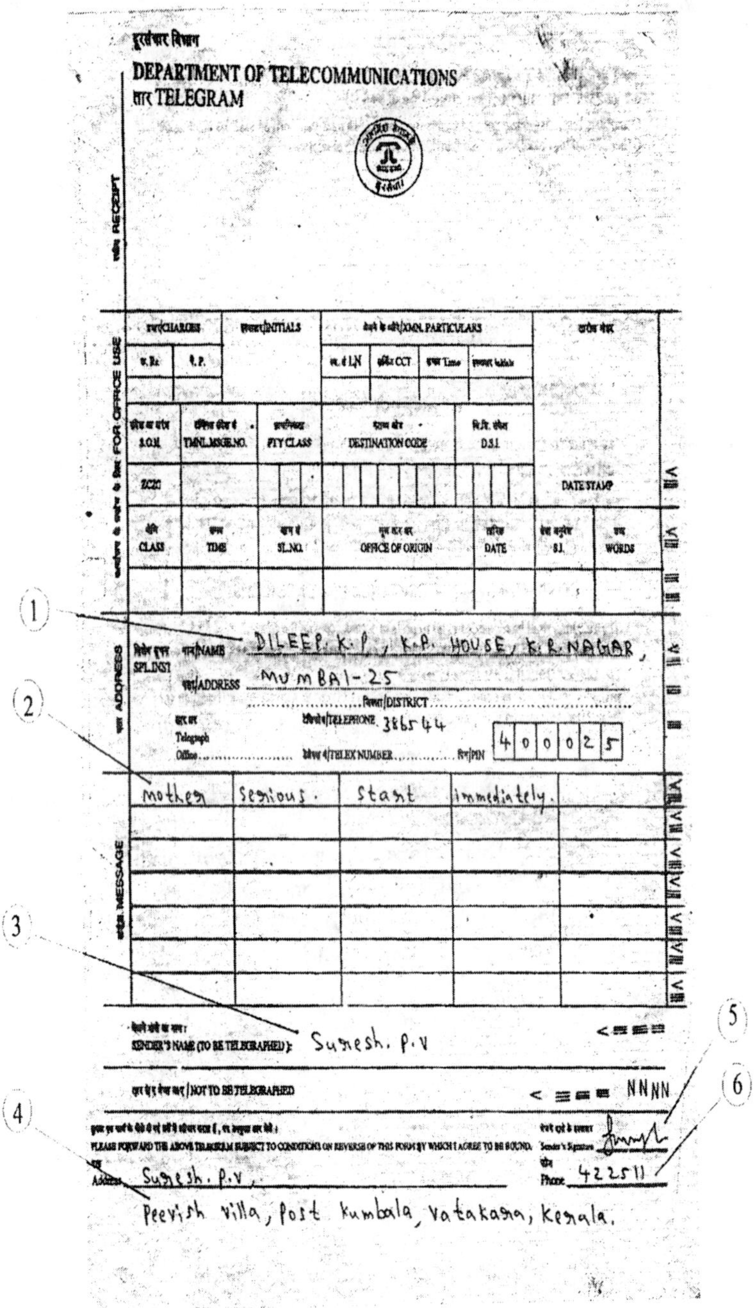

दूरसंचार विभाग
DEPARTMENT OF TELECOMMUNICATIONS
तार TELEGRAM

RECEIPT

FOR OFFICE USE

CHARGES		INITIALS	XMN. PARTICULARS				DATE STAMP
Rs.	P.		LN	CCT	Time	Initials	
S.O.M.	TMNL.MSGE.NO.	PTY CLASS	DESTINATION CODE		D.S.I.		
ZCZC							
CLASS	TIME	SL.NO.	OFFICE OF ORIGIN	DATE	S.I.	WORDS	

ADDRESS

SPL.INST NAME DILEEP. K.P, K.P. HOUSE, K.R. NAGAR,
ADDRESS MUMBAI-25
DISTRICT
Telegraph Office TELEPHONE 38644
TELEX NUMBER PIN 400025

MESSAGE

mother	serious.	start	immediately.	

SENDER'S NAME (TO BE TELEGRAPHED): Suresh. P.V

NOT TO BE TELEGRAPHED NNNN

PLEASE FORWARD THE ABOVE TELEGRAM SUBJECT TO CONDITIONS ON REVERSE OF THIS FORM BY WHICH I AGREE TO BE BOUND. Sender's Signature

Address Suresh. P.V, Peevish Villa, Post Kumbala, Vatakara, Kerala. Phone 422511

(1) (2) (3) (4) (5) (6)

Note:

1. Write full address, Pin Code and telephone number of the person to whom the message is sending.
2. Write message in brief. Write on word in one box. You may use code numbers of standard phrases instead of message in full length. This saves money. Code numbers and the message it convey is given at th:: bottom.
3. Write your name.
4. Write your address.
5. Put your signature.
6. Write your phone number, if any.

Phrases for Inland Greeting Telegrams.

Code No.	*Message*
1.	Heartiest Dewali Greetings.
2.	Id Mubarak.
3.	Heartiest Bijoya Greetings.
4.	A Happy New Year to you.
5.	Many Happy Returns of the Day.
6.	Heartiest congratulations on the New Arrival.
7.	Congratulations on the Distinction conferred on you.
8.	Best wishes for a Long and Happy Married Life.
9.	A Merry Christmas to you.
10.	Hearty congratulations on your success in the examination.
11.	Best wishes for a safe and pleasant journey.
12.	Hearty congratulations on your success in Election.
13.	Many thanks for your Good Wishes which I/We Reciprocate Most Heartily.
14.	Congratulations.
15.	Loving Greetings.
16.	May Heaven's Choicest Blessings be showered on the young couple.
17.	Wish you both a Happy and Prosperous Wedded Life.
18.	Kind Remembrances and all Good Wishes for the Independence Day.
19.	Sincere Greetings for the Republic Day. Long Live the Republic.
20.	My Heartiest Holi Greetings to you.

21. Wishing the Function every success.
22. Many Thanks for your kind message of Greetings.
23. Best Wishes for your success in the Examination.
24. Best Wishes for your success in the Election.
25. Blessings to the Newly Married Couple.
26. Heartiest Pongal Greetings.
27. Heartiest Gurpurb Greetings.
28. Greetings on the occasion of Paryusham. A Day of Universal forgiveness.
29. Heartiest Onam Greetings.
30. Best Wishes for your Wedding Anniversary.
31. Wish you a Happy Retired Life.
32. Wish you a Speedy Recovery.
33. Heartiest Ugadi Greetings.
34. Congratulations on your victory.
35. Wish you a Happy Bihu.
36. A Happy Easter.
100. My Deepest Condolence.

EXERCISE:

Q. 1. Send a telegram to your uncle wish a happy Independence day. You may use code no. for message.

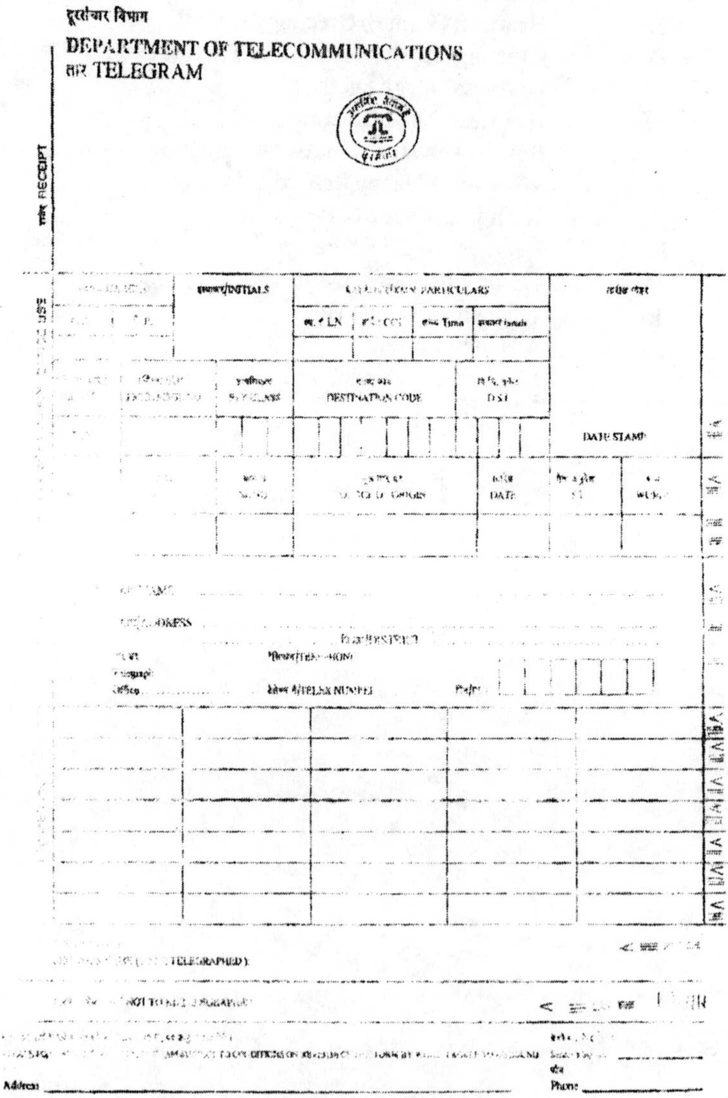

दूरसंचार विभाग

DEPARTMENT OF TELECOMMUNICATIONS

तार TELEGRAM

INITIALS

PARTICULARS

DESTINATION CODE

DATE STAMP

DATE

TELEGRAPHED

Address

Phone

Q. 2. Send a telegram to your brother asking him to return immediately because your mother is serious.

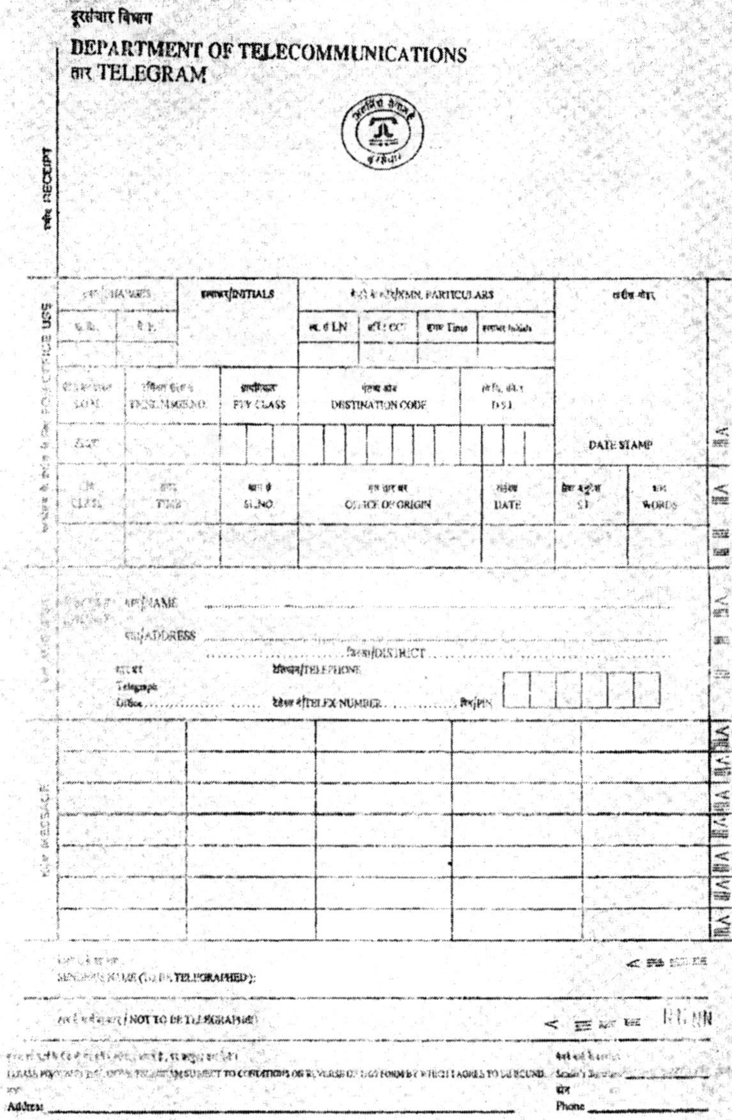
दूरसंचार विभाग
DEPARTMENT OF TELECOMMUNICATIONS
तार TELEGRAM

INITIALS | PARTICULARS | LN | Time
DESTINATION CODE
DATE STAMP
TIME | SL.NO. | OFFICE OF ORIGIN | DATE | WORDS

NAME ....
ADDRESS ....
DISTRICT ....
Telegraph Office .... TELEPHONE / TELEX NUMBER .... PIN

SENDER'S NAME (TO BE TELEGRAPHED):
(NOT TO BE TELEGRAPHED)

Address ____________ Phone ____________

7

Acknowledgement

Acknowledgement card is used to send registered postal article. If it is attached to the registered article, it would get back with the signature of addresee. This ensures proper delivery. It has two sides. A sample, showing how to fill it, is given overleaf.

Side – A

आर०पी०–54/R. P.-54

भारतीय डाक विभाग
DEPARTMENT OF POST , INDIA
प्राप्ति स्वीकृति/ACKNOWLEDGEMENT

रजिस्ट्री–पत्र/पार्सल प्राप्त हुआ
Received Registered Letter/Parcel/ ____________

क्रमांक/No. ____ तारीख/Dated ____ का/of ____

*बीमे का मूल्य रुपयों में ____________
*Insured for Rupees ____________

पाने वाले ____________
Addressed to ____________

____

को/on ____________

हस्ताक्षर और नाम/Signature and Name

वितरण डाकघर की तारीख–मोहर
Date-stamp of office of delivery

* अनावश्यक को काट दिया जाए
* Strike out if not relevant

8

Money Order Form

This is a money order form. It is used to send money through post office. Fill it up and give it to the M.O. Clerk alongwith money. See the example given on overleaf and learn how it is filled.

M.O. - 6

DEPARTMENT OF POST, INDIA
MONEY ORDER

PAY RUPEES ....

Rs. ....

To ....

....

.... PIN [| | | | |]

Sender's Signature

(FOR OFFICIAL USE ONLY)

M.O. No. .... Date ....

Rupees ....

....

Rs. ....

Combined Oblong Stamp — Assistant Postmaster

Received Rupees ....

....

Round M.O. Stamp — Signature of Payee

Signature of witness / identifier

Oblong Stamp — Signature of paying official

M.O. ACKNOWLEDGEMENT

M.O.No. .... Date ....

(Sender's Name & Address)

....

....

....

....

PIN [| | | | |]

Received Rupees ....

.... on ....

Date Stamp — Signature of Payee

(Space for Communication)

M.O. 8

DEPARTMENT OF POST, INDIA

MONEY ORDER

(1) Rupees: Two hundred

(2) 200/-

(3) To The manager, Prakash Book Depot, Bara Bazar, Bareilly, U.P State

(4) Rajeevan

Signature of witness / identifier

Oblong Stamp

Signature of paying official

M.O. ACKNOWLEDGEMENT

M.O.No.................................... Date....................................

(Sender's Name & Address)

(5) M. Rajeevan,
"Paradise"
P.O. Bangalore University,
Bangalore.

PIN

Received Rupees....................................

.... on....................................

Date Stamp

Signature of Payee

(Space for Communication)

(6) Please send me one copy of 'Dictionary of Shakespearian References'
M. RAJEEVAN, "PARADISE", P.O. BANGALORE UNIVERSITY, BANGALORE.

Note:

1. Write the letters the amount that you are sending.
2. Write in figures the amount that you are sending.
3. Write full address of the person to whom you are sending the amount.
4. Put ycur signature.
5. Write your address.
6. Write the message that you are wishing to send to the person who receives your money.

EXERCISE

Q. 1. Send fifty rupees to the following address for getting an application and prospectus for B.E. Course.

Principal, Oxford Engineering College, Jaipur - 20.

M.O. - 8

DEPARTMENT OF POST , INDIA
MONEY ORDER

PAY RUPEES ....

Rs. ....

To ....

....

.... PIN

Sender's Signature

M.O. No. .... Rupees ....

....

....

Rs. ....

(FOR OFFICE USE ONLY)

Con... Oblong Stamp .... Assistant .... Postmaster

Received Rupees ....

....

Round M.O. Stamp

Signature of Payee

Signature of witness / Identifier

Oblong Stamp

Signature of paying official

M.O. ACKNOWLEDGEMENT

M.O.No. .... Date ....

(Sender's Name & Address)

....

....

....

.... PIN

Received Rupees ....

.... on ....

Date Stamp

Signature of Payee

(Space for Communication)

Q. 2. Send Rs. 1000 to your aunt in Simla for her medical treatment. Her address is, Mrs. Savitri, Rajendra Bhavan, Simla - 11

M.O. - 8

DEPARTMENT OF POST , INDIA
MONEY ORDER

PAY RUPEES ....

Rs. ....

To ....

....

.... PIN [ ][ ][ ][ ][ ][ ]

Sender's Signature

(FOR OFFICIAL USE ONLY)

M.O. No .... Date........................

[ ] Rupees........................

....

Rs. ....

Commission Oblong Stamp Assistant Postmaster

( ) Received Rupees........................

....

Round M.O. Stamp Signature of Payee

[ ] Signature of witness / Identifier

Oblong Stamp Signature of paying official

M.O. ACKNOWLEDGEMENT

M.O.No.. Date........................

(Sender's Name & Address)

....

....

....

.... PIN [ ][ ][ ][ ][ ][ ]

( ) Received Rupees........................

.... on........................

Date Stamp Signature of Payee

(Space for Communication)

9

Postal Order

Indian Postal Order is another mode of money transfer from one place to another using postal service. Go through this section and find how to fill a postal order.

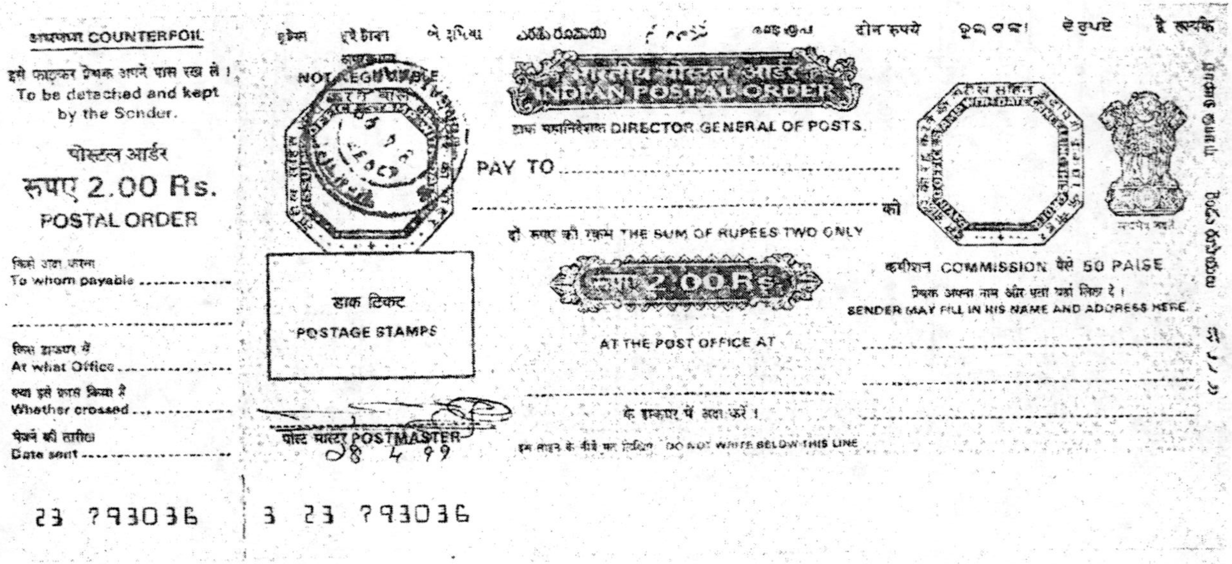
प्रतिपर्ण COUNTERFOIL
इसे फाड़कर प्रेषक अपने पास रख ले।
To be detached and kept by the Sender.
पोस्टल आर्डर
रुपए 2.00 Rs.
POSTAL ORDER
To whom payable
At what Office
Whether crossed
Date sent
23 793036
NOT NEGOTIABLE
डाक टिकट
POSTAGE STAMPS
पोस्ट मास्टर POSTMASTER
3 23 793036
भारतीय पोस्टल आर्डर
INDIAN POSTAL ORDER
DIRECTOR GENERAL OF POSTS.
PAY TO
THE SUM OF RUPEES TWO ONLY
रुपए 2.00 Rs.
AT THE POST OFFICE AT
DO NOT WRITE BELOW THIS LINE
COMMISSION पैसे 50 PAISE
SENDER MAY FILL IN HIS NAME AND ADDRESS HERE

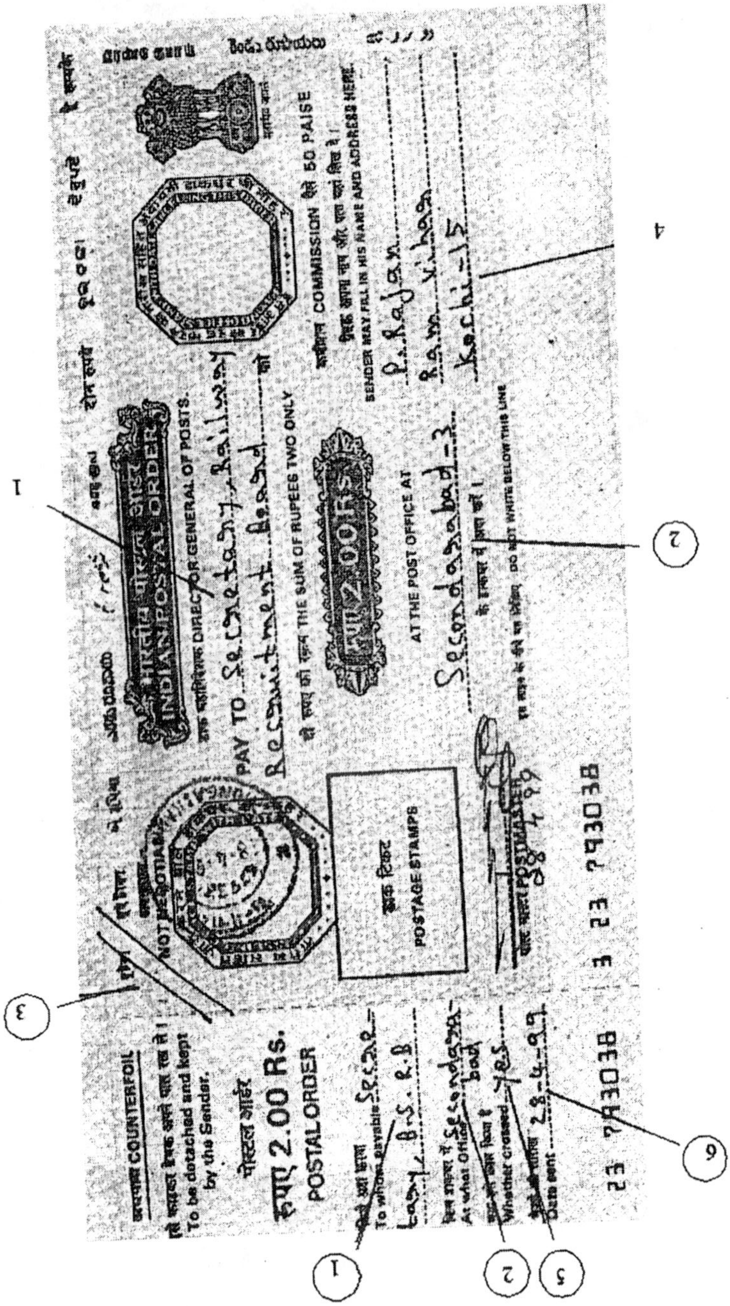
COUNTERFOIL
To be detached and kept by the Sender.
2.00 Rs.
POSTAL ORDER
To whom payable
At what Office
Whether crossed
Date sent
NOT NEGOTIABLE
POSTAGE STAMPS
POSTMASTER
INDIAN POSTAL ORDER
PAY TO
THE SUM OF RUPEES TWO ONLY
AT THE POST OFFICE AT
COMMISSION 50 PAISE
SENDER MAY FILL IN HIS NAME AND ADDRESS HERE.
DO NOT WRITE BELOW THIS LINE
1
2
3
4
5
6

Q. 2. Prepare a uncrossed Postal Order in favour of Secretary, Union Public Service Commission, New Delhi.

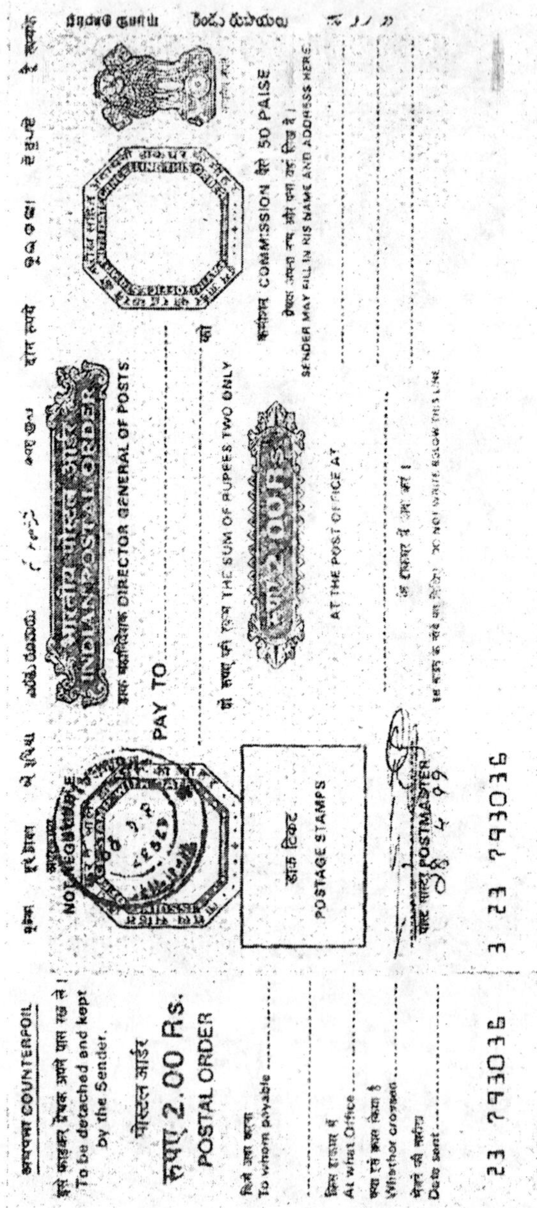
COUNTERFOIL
To be detached and kept by the Sender.
रुपए 2.00 Rs.
POSTAL ORDER
To whom payable ....
At what Office ....
Whether crossed ....
Date sent ....
23 793036

NOT NEGOTIABLE
INDIAN POSTAL ORDER
DIRECTOR GENERAL OF POSTS
PAY TO ....
THE SUM OF RUPEES TWO ONLY
COMMISSION 50 PAISE
SENDER MAY FILL IN HIS NAME AND ADDRESS HERE.
POSTAGE STAMPS
AT THE POST OFFICE AT ....
POSTMASTER
DO NOT WRITE BELOW THIS LINE
3 23 793036